Voices of Vietnamese Boat People

VOICES OF VIETNAMESE BOAT PEOPLE

Nineteen Narratives of Escape and Survival

Edited by
Mary Terrell Cargill *and*
Jade Quang Huynh

McFarland & Company, Inc., Publishers
Jefferson, North Carolina, and London

Library of Congress Cataloguing-in-Publication Data

Voices of Vietnamese boat people : nineteen narratives of escape
    and survival / edited by Mary Terrell Cargill and Jade Quang Huynh.
        p.   cm.
    Includes index.

    ISBN-13: 978-0-7864-0785-9
    (softcover : 50# alkaline paper) ∞

    1. Vietnamese Americans — Biography.   2. Refugees — United
States — Biography.   3. Refugees — Vietnam — Biography.
I. Cargill, Mary Terrell, 1945–   II. Huynh, Jade Ngoc Quang,
1957–
E184.V53 V63   2000
973'.049592'00922 — dc21
[B]   99-86302

British Library Cataloguing-in-Publication data are available

Front cover photograph courtesy of UNHCR/B. Boyer

Manufactured in the United States of America

McFarland & Company, Inc., Publishers
  Box 611, Jefferson, North Carolina 28640
  www.mcfarlandpub.com

To Mary Wrenetta McCain
for her advice and encouragement

Acknowledgments

The contributions of Gail Spake and Stephen W. F. Berwick are gratefully acknowledged.

Table of Contents

Preface

In 1995 in a college sophomore literature class I asked my students to write about their relationship with the natural world. As I walked about the classroom peering over the students' shoulders, I found that they made frequent references to the ocean's beauty and the memories they had of summer trips to the beach. However, student Duyen Nguyen's paragraph was different. In it she described the ocean as terrifying—a place associated with darkness, violence, and separation. I asked Duyen if she would be willing to tell her story to the rest of the class. In moving and vivid terms, she told the rapt students of her nighttime escape from Vietnam by boat. She described her journey, without any family members, to Thailand and the rigors of a refugee camp.

In spring 1996, I had Duyen's younger sister Lan in the same course, as well as another Vietnamese student, Ai-Van Do. Toward the end of the course the three of us talked about the possibility of committing their stories of escape and survival to paper. Ai-Van said that she had already planned to write her family's story and asked if I would be willing to edit it. Her question awakened in me the possibility of putting together a collection of Vietnamese survival narratives.

I soon discovered, however, that putting together such a collection would not be easy. When I met with a Memphis Vietnamese leader, he said it would be difficult to complete such a project because he felt that too few refugees had the ability and the confidence to express themselves adequately in written English. He also believed that most Vietnamese Americans would be unwilling to tell their stories because they wanted to put their terrible experiences behind them.

1

I spoke next with Judy Powell, Memphis Services Coordinator of Refugee Resettlement for Catholic Charities. Judy's response to the project was entirely enthusiastic. She thought that significant good could come from recognizing the sufferings and triumphs of the Vietnamese community. With Judy's encouragement, I moved ahead with the project and completed the first fourteen narratives.

In spring 1998, I asked Jade Quang Huynh to be my coeditor and to help me finish the collection. Of the nineteen narratives now included, Ai-Van Do, Suzanne Tran, and Jade all wrote their stories. The other sixteen are based on interviews. The last story describes Jade's return to what had been Leam Sing Refugee Camp in Chanthabury, Thailand. Jade's complete escape and survival story, *South Wind Changing*, was published in 1994 by Graywolf Press and has received many favorable reviews. I am grateful to Jade for his contributions.

I offer this book as a tribute to the courage and endurance of the Vietnamese boat people.

Mary Terrell Cargill
Christian Brothers University, Memphis
January 2000

Introduction

On April 10, 1975, the Hanoi government of North Vietnam took over the South and immediately pulled down the bamboo curtain. The government implemented a merciless policy against the Southerners. This policy created chaos: family breakups, total loss of means, and executions without trial. Day-to-day living became increasingly difficult and dangerous. In the first of the nineteen narratives included in this volume, Ai-Van Do explains how "illiterate 'doctors' from the war zones and the North had replaced the hospital's former doctors. ... [These new 'doctors'] had neither instructions nor medicine." Ai-Van's parents were so frightened of the authorities, "they lived as if they were snails inside their shells and did not dare go anywhere to meet anyone." In his narrative, Hung Truong tells how he became both mother and father to his three younger brothers. When his grandfather offered him money to buy clothes for New Year's, he responded with a question: "I need new clothes? What for? My life is nothing. I don't have a mom. I don't have a father. I need clothes? What for?"

Religious persecution, brainwashing, and total control of speech were hallmarks of the period. Ha Nguyen describes how a policeman who didn't like you might "just make up a reason and take you to jail.... Once the police thought a lady who lived next door to us knew something about a theft. They beat her even though she was pregnant, and she lost the child. She didn't know anything." Everywhere the concentration camps, known officially as "reeducation camps," had been built, and "New Economic Zones" were established. This brutality was most severe toward intellectuals and people who had been tied to the former Southern government. The result of this policy was the refugee exodus.

Thousands and thousands of rickety boats sailed out of South Vietnam's rivers, creeks, and beaches into the South China Sea. On the voyages, the refugees faced starvation, pirates, rapists, and the challenges of nature. On his boat, Hung Truong survived a downpour: "The rain was driving real hard. It was like somebody took sticks and beat my face real hard." Ai-Van's father wrote on day five of his sea diary: "It was as though we were in a large valley surrounded by many high mountains of water. All of us still think that perhaps we will die here." Hung Lang recounts his actions after being at sea many days without food or water: "I wrote a letter, put it in a bottle, and threw it overboard, hoping someone would find it and let my family know that I had died on the sea." No statistics exist on the number of boat people who traveled the waters outside Vietnam or how many died at sea. But no one doubts that the South China Sea became a vast burial ground.

Although the lucky ones who made it to the refugee camps were confronted with an uncertain future, they had a good chance of survival. Minh Nguyen's parents learned the ways of survival: "You might trade an egg for a cigarette," depending on your need. Lan Nguyen wound up in a Thai camp, where she and her family lived in fear of the guards: "If they saw a young girl and they wanted to make her sleep with them, they might beat her if she resisted." However, not all was bleak in the camps. Binh Le watched television for the first time in a Malaysian camp: "There were two 20-inch color televisions for about 10,000 people.... I loved it."

The nineteen people who tell their stories in this volume all eventually made it to the United States where they had to adapt to a different economic system and become part of an alien society. Like them, thousands of other Vietnamese refugees also had to adjust to a new status in the framework of U.S. society.

In the 1990s, after two decades of deterioration on many fronts, the Hanoi government's policies slowly began to change. The government started allowing Vietnamese refugees to return to the country for visits. Hanoi began to solicit foreign tourists and businesses and to normalize relations with the U.S. government. The Vietnamese government wanted foreign currency and hoped to end its isolation from the world community. Although many refugees went back to Vietnam to visit, some understandably hesitated to return to their homeland and confront what they had left behind. Nhan T. Le had high expectations about her visit home, but when she arrived she found out how poverty played a part in the new society, especially in the lives of children. In her home district, she witnessed children picking up plastic in a contaminated river to exchange for food. She met an old acquaintance and saw how such a short time had aged her friend, physically and mentally.

Hung Nguyen returned to Vietnam with his wife, Thu Ha Vo, for the first time in 1995. Since they had no children, Hung and Thu Ha decided: "Maybe God planned it that way. Not having children during the last 17 years gave us the time and money to support the brothers and sisters and nieces and nephews in Vietnam.... Eventually 22 relatives will be living here with me and my wife. Each of them should be with us in about 14 months. That's our plan." Hung's words highlight two themes that resound through all the narratives: indomitable spirit and love of family.

The Vietnam War Memorial is a revered monument in Washington, D.C. Perhaps there should be a memorial to the Vietnamese boat people as well.

Chapter 1

Simple Map, Small Compass, Three Flashlights

In 1998 **Ai-Van Do** graduated from Christian Brothers University in Memphis and went on to study at East Tennessee State University–Quillen College of Medicine in Johnson City, Tennessee. She married in January 1999.

My father, Minh Tan Do, was born into a middle-class Vietnamese family who made their living selling dry goods. He grew up in the small, coastal market town of Song Cau, located in the northern part of Phu Yen Province in central Vietnam, about 13° north of the equator. This is a beautiful region with soaring mountains in the west and white sandy beaches in the east. An unclouded river winds its serpent body along the shaded banks lined with coconut trees. But his country's loveliness would soon contrast sharply with the bitterness and anguish my father was to face.

Many problems began to creep into my father's life the year his mother died. He was only 16, and life became increasingly difficult. My grandfather had to work hard to feed and care for his five children. After my father finished high school, he joined the South Vietnamese Navy as a second-class petty officer. Although he wanted to continue his education at the university studying literature and modern languages, too little money and his duty to his country in wartime prevented him from doing so.

Unlike my father, my mother, Ai-Hang Thi Le, came from a very poor family in Qui Nhon City in a province neighboring Phu Yen. When she was only three years old, her mother died of heart disease, leaving her father to raise six children alone. To make life easier, he remarried. Since there was so little money in the household, my mother was only able to finish the tenth grade. Then she completed a nursing course and became a civil servant.

In February 1972, my father went to Qui Nhon City to serve with the Naval Logistical support unit. There he met and befriended my mother's elder brother, who was also a seaman, and soon met and fell in love with my mother. The following year my parents married.

When the Communist forces invaded South Vietnam on April 30, 1975, they had succeeded in their domination of all Vietnam. It was as if a black curtain had fallen on our country. All of former South Vietnam fell into despair. All the military and naval forces dispersed, and most of them surrendered to the Communist forces. My father also presented himself at the Communist naval headquarters to avoid trouble from the new government. My parents then left Saigon to return to my father's home town of Song Cau, with both joy and sorrow in their hearts. They were joyful because the war was over but sad about leaving Saigon, where they had had so many happy moments together. In their hearts, they knew that they might never see Saigon again. They worried about beginning a new life, not knowing how the Communists would act.

The Communists sent my father to a camp in the mountains to be "reeducated" and to do hard labor. During this time much sorrow and shame burdened my father. My mother was living with my father's family while he was away, and she was pregnant with me. After the government declared my father officially re-educated, they released him. Meanwhile my mother went to Qui Nhon City for the birth of their first child.

My parents thought that because the hospital in Qui Nhon City was large, my mother would have better care there than she would in the hospital in my father's small town of Song Cau. After the delivery, she lay sick in the hospital for more than a month and was nearly paralyzed on one side of her body. Others had to attend to all her personal needs. Because new, illiterate "doctors" from the war zones and the North had replaced the hospital's former doctors, they could do nothing for her. They had neither instructions nor medicine.

My father had to ask permission from the local constabulary to go to Qui Nhon City to care for my mother and me. Every day he went to the hospital to help my mother, and at night he returned to his father-in-law's house to care for me. Because his mother and two sisters had died in the same hospital, he feared that my mother would also die. Even if my mother survived, he was afraid that she might remain paralyzed forever.

Fortunately, my mother recovered from her illness, and we went back to Song Cau to begin our independent lives as a little family. Instead of living with my grandfather, uncles, and aunts, we built a small hut by the river's edge in my grandfather's beautiful coconut grove. It was from this place that God would later give us the opportunity to organize a successful escape. For a time in Song Cau and the rest of Vietnam, the Communists did not take over personal property. Instead, they urged everyone to increase production to create prosperity for the nation. They urged fishermen to catch more fish and farmers to cultivate idle lands in the mountainous regions. Under the "New Regime," everyone had to work hard. The slogan of the day was "Labor is the glory."

Because my parents had served under the former government, they had to work more strenuously than others. They had to prove to the Communist authorities that they had "awakened" and, thus, could feed themselves. My parents worked at two jobs during this period, fishing and farming, and they had no training for either.

My parents' fishing equipment consisted of a small sailboat, several nets, and some fishing rods they had bought cheaply from fishermen. Every night my father would row his boat along the shore for fishing, and at daybreak he would return with a basket of small fish. Then, while he cared for me, my mother would take the fish to the market to sell. With the little money she earned, she would buy a little rice and other food for our family. Going from city nurse to country fishmonger was difficult for my mother at first because many people teased her and called her "fishwife." With my father's encouragement, she gradually adapted and accepted her new role.

Each day after my mother came back from the marketplace, my father would mount his rickety bicycle and head for his job as a farmer. Our family had no field for rice planting, so my father cultivated a slope of barren land near my great-uncle's house. Since my mother's health was still fragile, my father worked alone, pulling up tree stumps and moving huge boulders as best he could. He terraced the slope into many levels and planted banana, breadfruit, and mango trees as well as beans, corn, sweet potatoes, and manioc. Manioc, a root with little nutritional value, was a staple food for people in many parts of Vietnam. In our area, many families mixed manioc with a small amount of rice for their meals. Other even poorer families ate manioc as a rice substitute because rice was more expensive. Although the people still grew rice, the Communist government was buying it at a very cheap price and sending it to North Vietnam. At first no one could understand why the government would do that. However, they learned later that the rice was being sent to Communist officials in the North.

Soon the new government became more severe and used collectivism for every type of production. The people did not own their fields, their boats, or any of the things they used to earn a living. The government ended private commerce and centralized all trades under a plan called "two-way commerce." This meant that fishermen and farmers, for example, had to sell their products to the government. In return, the government would sell them needed items such as fuel, rice, clothes, meats, and medicine. However, this "two-way commerce" provided the people with too little for a productive life.

The Communists had also confiscated the goods of former businesspeople. Therefore, people who still had money could not buy freely. Some of these businesspeople had hidden their goods and would sell to the people at inflated prices. In the cities, the Communists forced many businessmen, soldiers, and civil servants of the former government to leave their homes and go to New Economic Zones. There the people would break new ground and begin farming. The new government confiscated the homes the people had been forced to leave.

The Communists stripped the people of all their basic freedoms. Of course, they dealt more severely with former soldiers and former civil servants such as my parents. Typically they forced such people to perform hard labor in the harsh mountain regions for several months a year. Because of rough treatment, the people felt as though the Communists were punishing them and getting revenge. Many people died from work-related accidents or malaria. They lived as if they were snails inside their shells and did not dare go anywhere to meet anyone. Now the people understood that their hopes for peace and joy would not be realized. They began to complain and to hope for a return of the former government, as well as a return of the resisting forces still believed to be hiding in the mountains. Any meetings automatically aroused suspicion from Communist officials, especially the Christian gatherings at churches because of the churches' anti–Communist sentiment. The government threatened to punish anyone suspected of being discontented or uncooperative. The people knew that such offenders would be either brainwashed or forced to do strenuous labor in the faraway mountain region, sometimes never to be heard from again.

Earlier, my grandfather had given my parents a small radio. With this radio they listened secretly to the "Source of Life," a religious program broadcast in Vietnamese nightly from Manila. This Christian program, with its message of salvation and hope, brought peace to my parents after each tiring day. Believing that there was truly a God somewhere in all the bitterness and destruction eased my parents' sorrow.

One night in late March 1976 after my parents had listened to the "Source of Life," they continued to listen to the broadcast of Voice of America to hear the world news. This night they learned about a group of Vietnamese refugees who had used a fishing boat to escape from Vietnam and travel across the sea in search of freedom. A foreign merchant ship had eventually rescued them. Later, my parents learned of others who had escaped the same way. With this door of hope opened, my mother and father began to discuss plans for escape. While working on a warship as a seaman, my father had learned a few basic navigational skills. The only problem was that we had no large fishing boat with a motor. But my parents did not dare to collaborate with other fishermen who were boat owners for fear that the others would report them to the authorities.

However, my father did not give up. He decided to confide in four others who felt the same about the government as he and who loved freedom as much as my parents. The group decided to try to reach the Philippines because of its reputation for welcoming refugees. The escape plan was daring. They would first gather fuel and food and then try to steal a boat. My father knew that stealing would anger God, but he hoped that God would forgive him because of his desperate situation.

Alone, my father rowed his small boat along the shore toward the mountains looking for a place to hide the food and fuel. Eventually he discovered a solitary spot covered by thickets, and there he made a safe storage place.

All those involved combined their money and bits of jewelry and slowly and secretly bought empty plastic containers for storing the food and fuel and other supplies. They bought these items at very high prices from fishermen who had more than enough supplies for their fishing. At night my parents' companions would carry the fuel by bicycle to the shore and hide it. My father pretended to row the boat as though he were fishing on the river, and when he saw their signal, he took the boat in closer to the shore to collect the fuel. Then he rowed the boat at night, crossing more than ten kilometers, to the hiding place on the bay. He had to be careful to avoid patrols. After hiding the fuel, he took the boat into deep waters and slept until dawn, when he would wake up to catch some fish and return home.

For three months my parents continued to do this. Our hiding place stored more than 600 liters of fuel, a quantity large enough for a 20-horsepower motor to take us to the Philippines. The group had completed the first part of the plan. Now my parents only had to prepare food and water, and of course, someone had to steal a boat. My father, however, would have nothing to do with the stealing of the boat; others were taking care of that.

My parents worried about this part. They dared not meet with their friends anymore for fear of the spying Communist constabulary. Because my parents did not hear from the others for several weeks, they began to fear that something was wrong. One morning my father rowed his boat to the hiding place to inspect the stores again. His heart sank when he discovered that all the fuel was gone. Who had found the fuel? Did the authorities know of their plans? Had their companions betrayed them? My parents could not find any answers, and the others in the group avoided them.

Later my parents learned that one of the others had sold the fuel to a fisherman. The reason given was that the man's wife had given birth, and they needed the money. At least the authorities knew nothing of the plan. Despite this setback, my parents began to hope again. They even paid their share and joined forces with another group who then cheated them out of their money. Despite all these disappointments, they did not lose hope.

On the surface my father was a "good citizen." He did not refuse any labor, he attended reeducation meetings, and he talked with others about the "very good policy of socialism" and about the happiness it would bring the people in the future. However, my parents were living double lives. Their minds were often in a dream world where they would escape to freedom. Although my mother often saw my father gazing out to the sea like a haggard man who had lost hope, both continued to pray that God would give them a chance to escape.

Then one day my parents decided to escape on their own, with no looking back. Using my mother's meager part-time earnings as a seamstress, they saved a little money again. They still did not know how they would manage, but they were determined to succeed somehow.

In early 1978, the government ordered everyone to register his or her principal occupation. This was to help the government set up communes in which people of like occupations lived together. Another purpose was to force certain people to relocate to the new, undesirable economic zones located in the barren mountain regions.

My parents registered their fishing occupation as their legal reason to live in the coastal region, although my father continued to tend his crops as well. My mother and father developed their fishing with the purchase of more nets and other equipment and a small, old, motorized fishing boat. The boat measured 5 meters, 90 centimeters long and 1 meter, 40 centimeters wide and had a 5-horsepower motor.

My parents registered their boat so that they could buy fuel more easily. My father worried about whether he could catch enough fish to meet the 2.5-ton-per-year requirement of the government's "two-way commerce" plan. My grandfather and other relatives objected to my parents' choice of fishing as their occupation because they wanted my parents to be farmers. They urged us to leave our small house and move to the family's ancestral house to help my great-uncle cultivate the land. My parents claimed that their poor health kept them from farming and that the farmers had to pay taxes and sell 90 percent of their produce to the government. They said it was much too difficult for them.

While my mother and father waited for the government to approve their choice of occupation and to issue the necessary fishing permits, they began to make repairs on the boat. My mother used what little money she had left to buy empty plastic containers and fuel from some fishermen. It was very expensive, but she managed to get together six cans of fuel and three empty containers. My parents buried the containers one at a time under the floor of our home, pulling up bricks and replacing them again. At that time, my parents did not think they were buying the fuel to escape in our small boat. They just wanted to store a necessary quantity of fuel to use gradually if they could not get approval right away from the authorities for their fishing.

Another amateur fisherman who lived in our hamlet was Thoi. Because he was a former soldier in the South Vietnamese Air Force and had received some of his training in the United States, Thoi was also spied on and suspected of rebellion by the Communists. He and my father often talked together, and my father found that they shared the same point of view. Thoi was longing for freedom and thought about escape too. However, he had only a small boat, smaller even than ours.

Many times Thoi pleaded with my parents to organize an escape using our boat, but they did not answer him. Although he was a clever mechanic and an experienced sailor, my parents feared that our small boat was not adequate for such a journey. Also, they were hesitant to collaborate with him because they believed his character was unstable. My mother and father agreed that they would use our boat as a means of escape only if our lives were in danger because of the local authorities.

Soon they repaired the boat and launched it. Since our neighbors were spying on us and suspicious of us, my father continued to fish, and my mother bought fuel every day with the money earned from selling the fish. She also dried sweet potatoes and cooked rice to store for any sudden need.

In mid–May 1978, the government forced my father to do hard labor for 15 days in a highland area very far from town. At that time I was three years old and lay sick in the hospital with typhoid fever. Because of my illness, the government allowed my father to go home to see me. When he arrived home, my mother told him that a large fishing boat had escaped several days before. My father was very sorry that he had not had an opportunity to connect with the escapees in order to leave with them.

At the same time a group of ten friends were acting secretly against the government. Because they feared being discovered by the government, they wanted to escape as soon as possible. The leader of this group, Nho, met with my father one evening to propose that he help them. The plan was for the group to buy a large fishing boat. Although the government would not permit boat owners to sell their boats, owners would sometimes just report boats stolen when they had actually been sold. The group would buy such a boat as well as food and fuel. My parents' part would be only to use our small boat to ferry supplies and people to the large boat in the open sea. My father would also have to navigate. My parents were willing, the weather was good, and the plans were progressing. Each Sunday night the group held secret meetings to discuss the progress being made. Both my parents earnestly hoped that their wish would come true, but turmoil was in their hearts.

One day some young boys in the group quarreled about money. My mother and father feared that the constabulary would learn of the secret plans and would never forgive such reactionary dealings. So my father stopped his work with Nho's group temporarily in order to avoid trouble. My parents still believed that God would protect us, and they prayed to Him.

My parents lived like fish in a fishbowl. They could not adapt to their present circumstances, and their future looked dark and uncertain. We were all emaciated and sick, especially my mother and I. My parents wanted to leave this prison of a country as soon as possible.

One evening in June 1978, while my parents were outside building a kitchen, a fisherman came by to tell them that Nho could not buy a boat because some members of the group had failed to pay their share. The man also warned that our secret plans were no longer a secret. Now that the constabulary knew our plans, my father feared persecution and punishment.

Later that night when we were listening to the "Source of Life," Thoi came to our house, his face pallid with fright, and he asked my mother to put out the light. In the dark he whispered to my father that he had just been ordered to go to a reeducation camp for an unspecified length of time. In the morning he expected my father to receive the same order. If they did not act immediately, the opportunity to escape would be lost. Thoi pleaded with my father to flee. My father argued that our boat was very small and old and that we had no food, water, or motor oil. Thoi countered that the weather was very good, that he would get some motor oil, and that we could prepare food and water now. During all this time, my mother and I were silent. Finally, my father turned to my mother and asked what she thought. Without any hesitation she answered: "It's up to you. Our daughter and I will follow you anywhere, although we may die." Thoi went home, and my parents went to town to buy food. Because it was late, they could get only rice paper, used to wrap fillings of meat and vegetables, plus some sugar and three cans of milk for me. After this my father carried water from my grandfather's house; thankfully, no one there knew what he was doing.

In the dark they groped about getting ready. My parents poured the water in the empty plastic containers and pulled up the floor bricks to get the six cans of fuel. My mother selected a few clothes for us. In the silence of the night, we were afraid our noise would attract the attention of the soldiers who were patrolling. My parents did not fear the departure as much as being caught during preparation.

By 1:30 that morning, our preparation was complete. Thoi came with a small bag on his back. It was the luggage his wife had prepared for him to go to the reeducation camp. He had secretly left his parents, his wife, and his son.

Thoi moved his 2.5-horsepower engine into our boat from his, thinking it could replace my father's engine if that one broke down. During the time they were transporting the supplies from the house to the boat, a young boy named Hung and his brother were bringing their nets to their boat to start fishing. But they did not notice us. Perhaps they thought we were just preparing to go fishing also. I was trembling all over when my mother carried me to the boat. My mother whispered: "My daughter, keep silent! If you cry, the Communists will catch us!" I obeyed.

Before my father started the engine, we looked at our home for the last time. I saw my little dog, To-To, standing at the water's edge, wagging his tail happily. He wanted to come along with us, poor dog. My mother and I lay on the bottom of the boat, while Thoi and my father guided it over a shallow place by getting out and pushing. Hung and his brother were also pushing their boat, but still they paid no attention to us. When the boat was in deep water, we began to run at full speed. As Thoi steered the boat, my father tended the engine. We were braving the waters in a fishing boat that was probably the smallest ever to sail over the sea. We had a simple map of the world, a small compass, and three flashlights to use for plotting our course and for signaling in the night.

Our small boat struggled with many dangers crossing over more than 800 miles from Vietnam to the Philippines during eight days and nights on the sea. During those eight days and nights on the water, my father somehow managed to keep a diary of our journey.

From My Father's Sea Diary

June 14, 1978, the first day of the voyage. By 6:00 A.M., the boat had departed from the bay, and our country with the green coconut trees and high mountains could barely be seen in the distance. The sky was clear and the sea was smooth. We changed direction to 90° east following the compass. A little before noon when a wind arose from the southwest, I put up the sail, and we gained speed. Later we came within sight of a large oil tanker from China. Many sailors on board looked at us with binoculars, but they did not stop to help us. Our first lunch on the sea consisted of sugar and rice paper that we softened by dipping into water. Ai-Van ate some dried sweet potatoes with a little milk, but she vomited. We are all afraid for her health. At midnight, the weather was still good. We spotted the direction-indicator lights of some ships that were rather far from our boat. Thoi asked me to signal an SOS, but they did not answer me.

June 15, day two. This morning at 8:00 there was not a ship in sight. We felt so all alone on the immense sea. The southwest wind blew heavily, making the sea rough and the boat swing violently, but this has not made us afraid yet. The sea calmed down this evening, and the moon is now shining in a clear sky.

June 16, day three. At 2:00 this morning we saw the lights of a ship and tried to run after it, but it was too far away to catch. A merchant ship passed by an hour later. Though Thoi and I used a white cloth and Ai-Hang waved her hat to try to signal the ship, it paid no attention to us. Everything around us became very quiet after the ship left. In the afternoon, the southwest wind blew, so I set the sail up to run the boat at full speed. By 8:00 that night, heavy rains began, and the wind blew terribly. About an hour later, we saw the lights of two ships headed south. Thoi flashed an SOS. The ships stopped, but when we approached them, they went away. Now it is midnight, and we are in the midst of a thunderstorm. A few minutes ago two other ships came near our boat, and again we signaled SOS. We had hoped to be saved. Ai-Hang even prepared our bundles. One of the ships flashed its signal light to find us, but it left us when it was only five meters away. Poor little Ai-Van waved to the sailors on board, but these ships also left. We could not understand why. Ai-Hang had begun to feel hopeless. We were worrying even more about the health of our little daughter.

June 17, day four. At 4:00 this morning I saw two ships, one heading south and the other northeast. Both of them stopped and waited for us to come near. It was daylight when we approached them, but they too turned away from us. Many dark clouds suddenly gathered in the sky. We knew another storm was approaching. As the wind began to blow, the sea grew rough and the rain poured upon us mercilessly. At 11:00 A.M., one spring of the engine broke, and we could no longer run it. This meant having to put up the sail. Ai-Hang embraced our little daughter and wept in fright. I prayed that God would give us the ability to repair the engine. As Thoi steered the boat, he sat smoking and rarely moved. Perhaps he was thinking of a solution to our engine problem. Ai-Hang and Ai-Van could not eat and had to lie weakly on the floor of the boat. At noon I took over the steering while Thoi tried to untie our boat's engine to replace it with his smaller engine, but it would not fit. Thoi angrily threw the small parts into the water. A seabird fearlessly skimmed above my head and wanted to settle on the sail. Thoi believed it was a very bad omen, and his face turned pale. It is evening now. The rain has stopped, and the sea is smooth and pleasant. The shining moon makes us all drowsy. Ai-Hang is dreaming. She looks as if she is going to step out of the boat, thinking the surface of the water is land.

June 18, day five. At 3:00 A.M., a large oil tanker stopped by us. It left right away, though we asked for help. Although ships have repeatedly ignored us when we so badly needed compassion, we still rely on the protection of God. The sea has been rough and stormy since this morning. At about 6 A.M., Thoi first bailed water from the boat, then tried to repair the engine. He tried using the flashlight springs to replace the broken engine spring, but it would not work. The wind was blowing forcefully today, making many high waves. Four unrecognizable bodies floated past us; they were probably other Vietnamese boat people. It was frightening to think that this seemingly infinite sea could at any time so easily swallow our tiny boat. It was as though we were in a large valley surrounded by many high mountains of water. All of us still think that perhaps we will die here. Thoi worked in silence, sometimes stopping to smoke or to sing a sad song. On this journey our lives have been held as if by a single silk thread. By 3:00 P.M., the engine's new spring was finally in place, but Thoi was afraid to start the engine because he did not believe it was strong enough. At last we dared to start it, and we ran slowly in the storm. That evening we saw no ships.

June 19, the sixth day of our voyage. This morning we discovered that we had no more motor oil and no more food or water. The time and the distance from the Philippines were as yet unknown to us. If we continued running without motor oil, we would ruin the engine. Our condition seemed hopeless. Surely death was near. At 3:00 P.M., God answered our prayers when a large ship stopped by on its way to Japan from Malaysia. Thoi waved an empty can to signal our need. The *Donna Maria* stopped to help us. Many sailors looked at us and started waving. When they heard Thoi say that we were headed for the Philippines, they laughed and then told us we weren't going in the right direction. When the captain asked us what we needed, we begged him to save us, but he could not because his government would not allow it. He seemed to be very sad telling us this news. Although the sailors on board the ship could not rescue us, they supplied us with motor oil, food, and water. Some Filipino sailors aboard gave us 75 pesos. The captain also gave us the right direction and the distance to the Philippines. After saying good-bye to our benefactors, we continued our voyage with new hope. What a wonderful afternoon it was! We delighted in a dinner of bread, canned meats, and canned drinks. Ai-Hang was very happy and had a good appetite. Ai-Van was fascinated with her first apple. The sea is now quiet.

June 20, day seven. At 3:00 A.M., another engine spring broke. We had to wait until daylight for repairs. To make matters worse, salt water had started to leak into our weathered boat. At daylight, Thoi got another spring from one of the flashlights to replace the broken one. It was our last spring. While Thoi repaired the engine, we put up the sail, and I steered the boat. Finally the spring was replaced, and we continued our journey with the boat running at full speed. We spotted a group of dolphins racing one another, which amused us greatly. At around 7:00 that evening, the sea became rough with the first of a series of storms. The wind was very strong, and high waves splashed water into the boat. Thoi steered while I bailed. All of us were soaked. By nightfall we had lost our bearings because we could not see the face of the compass. We were trembling with cold. Earlier we met some ships passing us, but we had no desire to stop them anymore.

June 21, day eight. The rain gradually stopped right before daylight. Thoi took control of the steering while I leaned my back against the side of the boat to sleep for a little while. Soon Thoi spotted a lighted region in the east. When Ai-Hang and I awoke, we were overjoyed to think it could be the lights of Manila. By 6:00 A.M., we were certain that today would be the last day of our voyage because we could clearly see many mountains and several islands. After breakfast the storms started again. High waves surrounded our small boat to frighten us one last time. It was cloudy and dark with strong winds blowing from the southwest, making it impossible to see land anymore. But by 10:00 the storm had subsided. We could see the Philippines more clearly with each passing moment. I said to Ai-Hang and Thoi: "We have survived! It is certain!" Thoi seemed rather sad. Perhaps he was thinking about his family in Vietnam. We wanted to meet a coast guard ship of the Philippines to present ourselves but saw no such ship. There were only two Filipino fishermen in their small boats. When Thoi asked them the way to Manila, they seemed afraid and asked if we carried guns. When we assured them that we had no guns, they stopped to give us directions and wished us well. The speed of their motorboat surprised us. It ran as if it were flying on the face of the sea. At noon we changed our clothes and ate lunch. My buttocks had sores from constant sitting to steer or mind the engine. We followed the fishermen's directions and saw some villages much like ours back in Vietnam. I began to miss my relatives, for I believed that we would now have no occasion to see them again. At 4:00 P.M., we spotted a harbor with many large ships. It turned out to be the Manila harbor. We struggled out of the boat and took our first walk on land after eight days during which we had struggled with death. Some policemen received us and took us to the Marivelles Police Station in Bataan. We stayed the night there. Many Filipinos came to visit us and welcome us, and the authorities gave us help. Throughout the journey, neither my wife nor my daughter was ever seasick, despite the fact that our boat had no cabin or anything else to protect them from the sun, the rain, or the salt water.

My family and I stayed in a refugee camp in Bataan for one year. Life here was not easy. We lived in a handmade shack built of pieces of scrap wood, and the Filipino government gave us barely enough rice per day to live on. My mother was most frustrated by the rats that came into our shack at night and bit our feet.

Though our lives in the camp were difficult, we were fortunate to receive news of our sponsorship to the United States by Oakhurst Baptist Church in Clarksdale, Mississippi. The missionaries James and Paulette Kellum, who were working in our camp, had grown to love us and had introduced our family to their church back home. We boarded the plane to America in June 1979.

Ai-Van Do with her paternal grandfather, Kiem Tan Do, at Song Cau, summer 1995.

Ai-Van's family during their second return trip to Vietnam, summer 1995.

Since then, I have been able to return to Vietnam twice, once with my father during the summer of 1993 and again with my entire family in the summer of 1995. Vietnam is a beautiful country. I love the land, the people, and the mountains. Although on the surface, Vietnam seems like an improving Third World country, it is still Communist-dominated and thirsty for freedom. My dream is to one day return to a free Vietnam, to see the smiles of a free people.

Chapter 2

The Miracle
of the Whirlpool

Hung Lang and his wife Thu Ha settled in Memphis with
their son and daughter. There the family became active with
the local Vietnamese Baptist Church, with Hung serving as
deacon and Thu Ha as a church committee member, and both
teaching Bible classes.

In 1975 after the Communists took over South Vietnam, they put all the
officers of the former South Vietnamese Army in jails. They called these
reeducation camps, but they were jails.

Because I'd been a second lieutenant in the army, they put me in jail
and moved me about five or six times to different camps. In these camps
they would make us come to class, where they talked bad about America
and South Vietnam. I was in these camps for almost three years, until 1977.

After this I wanted to go back to my family in Saigon. My wife and
I weren't married yet. I had met her when I was working for the army in
Camau in the southern tip of Vietnam. We married on October 22, 1978,
and lived under communism for about five years. During that time we had
a son and a daughter. When I got out of the camps, I could not do anything with my life. Every week I had to go to the local government and
report what I did and where I went during the week. The government con-
trolled everything. I couldn't work for any company because I had been in
the South Vietnamese Army.

Also, my wife lived in Camau, and I lived in Saigon. I tried to go to
her town to live, but the government wouldn't let me. Sometimes my wife

would come to Saigon, but mostly we lived in two separate cities. Even though I couldn't see my kids often, they knew me. They were good children. At night they would say their prayers without my wife reminding them. How could I take care of my children that way? I couldn't find a job. So all these problems were why I planned to escape.

There was also the problem of religion. The Communists gave us a lot of trouble when we went to church in Vietnam. That is another reason we wanted to escape.

When I got out of the reeducation camp, I was broke, but God opened a way for me. I agreed to pay some of the money for the escape before we left Vietnam and the rest when we came to America. An uncle had promised us a large boat with everything on it, but he cheated us because what we got was a small boat with only a little food, water, and gas.

On April 20, 1984, we left from Camau, which is not quite on the coast, and went down to the country's southern tip, where about 22 of us got on an open boat. There were eight in our family: myself, my wife, my mother-in-law, my two kids, and my wife's three nieces. Including us, there were 11 Christians on the boat. A few times after we left, the motor broke down. I felt it was not safe to continue and wanted to go back, but the rest of them wouldn't let me. Really I knew we couldn't go back because I remembered my friend, another second lieutenant, who had tried to escape through Cambodia. They caught him, put him in jail, and killed him. I knew I couldn't go back. Eventually we got the motor working again. At the time I had no idea it was so far to Indonesia.

None of us had any experience on the sea, but the seas in April are usually pretty calm. After a few days out, my kids were hungry and thirsty. My wife held them in the back of the boat and prayed. Then I sat down, and she and I prayed. Then God let us have a real hard rain. This let the children live a few more days. On the eighth day out my three-year-old daughter died, on the ninth my four-year-old son died, and on the tenth my wife's smallest niece died. After her niece's death, everyone lay down on the boat. We couldn't do anything. We were helpless. I asked God why things had happened this way. We hadn't escaped for our future, but for the kids' future.

At that time it looked like a heavy rain would come, and we prayed that God would give us rain, but we couldn't get any. I asked God, "Why didn't you give us any water when we prayed?" But later I thought that if we had gotten a heavy rain, maybe the boat would have been upset, and everyone would have died.

One of the worst things that happened to us while we were on the

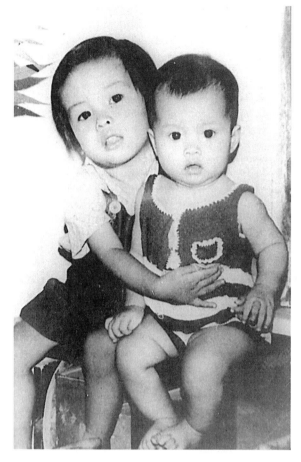

Hung Lang's son, Vi Hung, and daughter, Anh Ha, who died at sea in April 1984.

sea was that we got caught in a whirlpool.* Our boat went round and round in this whirlpool near the Gulf of Thailand for about two days. When we first got in it we were on the outer large circle, but the circle got smaller as we were pulled toward the center. We just held onto the boat because we were so scared. After we got to the refugee camps, we heard that almost all the boats that got caught in whirlpools had been lost.

It was Easter season, and the Christians on the boat were praising God. Then somehow we broke free of the whirlpool. After this we started singing whatever hymns we could remember and other Vietnamese songs. Two young ladies in the boat were converted when they saw how God's power on the sea had saved us from the whirlpool. We were told in the

*Dr. Eric Wolanski of the Australian Institute of Marine Science writes that he is "not aware of detailed studies of these eddies off Cape Camau; mathematically though, they can be expected. They can also be expected from comparison with areas elsewhere which have been studied. These eddies will not suck boats underwater, but they may keep boats in the same area for long periods" (e-mail: July 30, 1997). Contact Dr. Wolanski at ericw@ibm590.aims.gov.au. Also of interest is an article in the New York Times (Sept. 2, 1997, B7) by Malcolm W. Browne, "Deadly Maelstrom's Secrets Unveiled," about the Moskstraumen maelstrom off the coast of Norway. Browne cites Dr. Bjorn Gjevick of the University of Oslo, whose recent study of the Moskstraumen shows that "the maelstrom has little effect on large vessels, partly because they avoid it. ... The maelstrom's main victims are fishermen in small boats."

Thu Ha Lang (second from left) in Galang (Indonesia) Learning Center, 1984.

camps that everyone who got caught in a whirlpool died. I don't know why we were saved.

After we got out of the whirlpool, everyone on the boat was tired, so we lay down in the boat and thought we were going to die. My wife began to sing some hymns to make us feel better. The people asked my wife to keep singing. When she sang, many fish came round my boat. Some dolphins jumped up in the water. When my wife stopped singing, the fish went away. When she sang again, they came back. The people on the boat wanted her to keep singing so that they could watch the fish. I was a Christian in Vietnam, but I was very weak. After my escape, my faith was stronger because I saw the power of God on the sea.

We were on the sea without food or water for about 13 days. Then I wrote a letter, put it in a bottle, and threw it overboard, hoping someone would find it and let my family know that I had died on the sea.

But God helped us. A fishing boat came by carrying about 13 people who had escaped. After they delivered these people to the refugee camp in Indonesia, the fishermen came back and let some of us get on their boat. We were on that boat another three days, for a total of 16 days on the sea. My wife and I were stronger than the others, but my mother-in-law looked really bad. The men in the other boat didn't want to take her with us because they thought she was dying. If their boat had come by only one

Hung and Thu Ha Lang, with Thu Ha's sister, Sue Vu, holding their son, An, at the Memphis airport, May 1985.

or two days later, my mother-in-law and an old man on our boat might have died. Happily, both survived.

The people on the fishing boat helped us go to an Indonesian camp. First, we stayed for a few days at a camp on a small island named Kuku. Then we were moved to Galang, Indonesia, where there were two camps, Galang I and Galang II. While we were at Galang II, my wife had Thien An, our son, and I thanked God for him. In Vietnamese, "Thien" means "God" and "An" means "grace," thus his name means God's grace.

At the Galang church, I was a committee leader and my wife was treasurer. She and I taught Bible school. We had a wonderful life in the refugee camp. After a year at Galang II, we went directly to the United States.

Now I am an American citizen. In some ways, life in the camp was better than life is here in the United States because in the camp I had a chance to help people. Every week I saw many people come to believe in God.

Meanwhile my father, back in Vietnam, had been sick a long time. I wasn't sure it was safe for me to go back to Vietnam, but I love my father, so I visited him in 1991. In 1995, after my second visit, my father passed

Hung and Thu Ha Lang with An and Bich in Memphis, 1997.

away, but my mother still lives there. In December 1996, my whole family went back and stayed three weeks.

Vietnam has changed a lot. There are many new buildings in Saigon. Also, they've changed the names of streets, which makes it hard to recognize where things were before 1975. Despite these changes, the life of the people is poorer now than before 1975.

Chapter 3

Stranger in the Rice Field, Whale in the Sea

Minh Nguyen's parents, Hien and Non Nguyen, his sister, Phi Phuong Thi, and his brother, Truc, settled in Memphis. Minh was an electrical engineering major at Christian Brothers University (CBU) and graduated in 1998. Finding employment in Atlanta, Georgia, he relocated to Covington, Georgia. Phi Phuong graduated in 1997 as valedictorian of her class at Craigmont High School. She and Truc both went on to study at CBU.

Before 1975, my father was an officer of the Republic of Vietnam. He graduated from the Vietnam National Military Academy and fought for the South in the war. After 1975, he was put in a reeducation camp at Phuoc Long City for three years. When he got out of the reeducation camp, he returned to our hometown of Ba Ria (Phuoc Le), just northeast of Vung Tau, and drove a three-wheeler called a "xe lam." It's the equivalent to a small bus here. My mom sold rice and other products in the market. My family could survive, but my parents knew their children had no real future in Vietnam.

Our family consisted of my parents, my younger brother and sister, and me. There was no one to sponsor us to come to the United States. We had only very distant relatives here, no aunts or uncles. We also had some distant relatives in Australia, but America was where we really wanted to go.

For us, there was no other way to get out of Vietnam but by boat. We made four attempts to escape before we got out successfully. During the second attempt, after we had traveled at night across wet rice fields, my mother fell into a deep ditch. She got bruises all over her body. When that attempt failed and we got back to Ba Ria, everyone asked her why she was so bruised. She had to lie and tell them she had fallen off her bike. Another time the government found out we were trying to leave and put my father in jail from August 1981 to August 1982.

In 1983, when we made our fifth attempt, I was nine years old. No one knew about the plans to escape, not even my grandparents. Usually when you leave, you have to pay up front to the captain, but somehow the captain of this boat said we didn't have to. Instead, he said, "If you make it, you can pay later." I don't know where that trust came from, but we did pay after we made it.

Instead of leaving from Ba Ria, we left from my aunt's little village of Ong Trinh. My family hid in a field of tall grasses at about 6:00 P.M., and at 10:00 the person who was to be in charge of the boat said for us to follow him. We went through jungle and forest and rice fields. While we followed the man in charge of the boat, my mom, Non Nguyen, carried my little brother, Truc. He was two years old. My father, Hien Nguyen, carried my five-year-old sister, Phi Phuong, on his back and held my hand. My mom fell many times. She told my dad she was too tired to go on, but my dad told her just to try to keep going, keep going. Phi Phuong kept saying: "I don't want to go. I don't want to go." But my parents told her to be quiet, and we kept walking. Some person we didn't even know appeared and helped my mother carry Truc. This man helped her until we got to the small boat.

Although this boat was supposed to carry only 10 people, we somehow managed to fit 20 of us in it. We were worried that the boat might tip over. We traveled down the Ong Trinh River for about two hours until we came to the big boat. One hundred and forty-six of us were crammed together onto this 100-passenger boat. Those in charge put all the women and children under the deck, and the men stayed on top. It still took us another two hours to get the rest of the way down the river and into the South China Sea. For the first few hours, we had calm waters, but after a while big waves came. Then I was seasick most of the time. Usually I was under the deck, but whenever we had clear weather, I would come out on top and watch dolphins. I remember seeing a whale too. The men talked about how lucky it was to see a whale.

Whenever it rained, my dad would go up on deck to catch the rainwater in plastic raincoats and then store it in plastic bottles. We had brought a lot of dried noodles, something like ramen. That's what we ate most of the time. There were times when we were low on food, but we had enough to survive.

My parents didn't know where the boat was going. They were depending on the captain to navigate. Wherever he wanted to go away from Vietnam was fine with them. One day after we left, we saw a boat far away. We could see a flag flying but weren't sure what kind it was. Usually, on the sea, any flag you see makes you happy, but when we approached it, we found out that it was a Thai pirate boat. We immediately headed in another direction, and the other boat started chasing us, but after a while it gave up.

After we'd been out about five days, we saw a big boat, like a cruise ship, from London. We asked them to take us on their ship, but they wouldn't. Instead, they gave us cigarettes, fuel, and food and showed us the direction to Malaysia. We kept going one more day and wound up in Singapore. But the officials in Singapore wouldn't accept us. Even so, we stayed one night among the boats there. The next morning we left, and at about 5:00 that evening stopped at a Malaysian oil refinery. They accepted us and let us off the boat. After all that time on the sea, seven days and seven nights, it seemed like the land was wobbling. When we got off the boat, we were taken to a big, empty building. Here the Malaysians took away everything we were carrying, including clothes and Vietnamese money, and threw it away. Then they told us to take a shower, and they gave us everything: clothes, shoes, and food. We spent two nights there. We never got back on the boat because the Malaysians sank it. They didn't want anyone else to steal the boat and use it for more people to escape from Vietnam.

We were moved from the oil refinery by bus to a little camp, where we stayed for two days and nights. Then they took us to Pulau Bidong by boat. We arrived at Pulau Bidong on Christmas Day, 1983. We thought everything there was good. We knew we were free. A lot of Vietnamese people we knew came to meet us, and we celebrated. Both my parents had relatives there.

We were on Pulau Bidong only three months because my dad brought all the necessary paperwork with him. Compared with most other people, we went through the system pretty fast.

I don't remember much about Pulau Bidong. Most of us kids just roamed around the camp. I do remember that if the camp authorities caught you fishing, they would shave your head as punishment. Some people just shaved their heads and went fishing anyway.

My mom stayed home to take care of the children while my dad studied English and worked in the camp office. Sometimes we would receive enough food for five adults, even though we had only two adults and three kids, so we shared what we didn't need with those who didn't have enough.

Minh Nguyen getting a certificate from his English teacher, September 1984, Philippines.

Hien and Non Nguyen, parents of Minh, Philippines, August 1984.

Minh Nguyen (center front) with his mother, Non (first on left, second row), and his father, Hien (second from right), before leaving the Philippines, October 1984.

There was also a lot of trading going on in the camp. For example, you might trade an egg for a cigarette. Some people had vegetable gardens, and some would bake and have a little market where they'd sell what they'd baked. One day I asked for a small cake, but we didn't have the money so my dad traded an egg for it.

After we left Pulau Bidong, we found out from the American delegation that we were being sent to Sungei Besi, a transit camp, where we stayed for about three months. After Sungei Besi we were sent to Morong, Bataan, Philippines, where the main thing we did was go to school. All of us but Truc went to school there. Also at Bataan we had a Buddhist temple where we could worship. We provided flowers and incense for the Buddha and food and water for the monks.

After six and a half months in the Philippines, Living Word Lutheran Church in Memphis agreed to sponsor us. We had never heard of Memphis, but we had heard of Elvis. The only places in the United States we had heard of were California, Washington, D.C., New York, and Texas. We were really happy that we were getting to leave the camp and come to America, and we will be forever in the debt of Living Word Lutheran for sponsoring us.

In summer 1994, after almost 11 years in the United States, I went back with my family to visit relatives in Ba Ria for one month. Before, when I remembered Vietnam, I thought everything was so big, but when I got back, everything seemed small and cramped. It was the opposite of what I had remembered. The country was torn up and not very productive. Also, there's not a lot of work available. I couldn't live there. No way.

When we left Saigon to come home, the customs officials told us to give them some money or they would find a reason we couldn't leave. Straight out they would say, "Give me $50 or you will be missing this suitcase or that camera." There is open corruption. One guy came up to us and said, "Give me $20 and I'll make sure you get through without any questions." Everyone knows the corruption is there, but no one does anything about it. Even though we were American citizens then, we were afraid they could keep us there and we could do nothing about it. In April 1997, my parents visited Vietnam again, this time to celebrate the death day of my father's father.

My parents say they would like to continue living in America. They are happier in America and know their children can get a better education here. On May 4, 1990, our wish came true, and all of us, parents and children, became American citizens.

Chapter 4

Gold Rings and Jeans

Lan Nguyen graduated from Christian Brothers University in 1998 with a major in chemistry. She was on the CBU tennis team. After working summers as a research assistant at St. Jude Children's Research Hospital, Lan went on to study medicine at University of Tennessee Medical School in Memphis. Lan is the younger sister of Duyen Nguyen, whose story follows, and a cousin to Ha Nguyen, whose story follows Duyen's.

I don't remember much that happened before I was about seven years old. What I remember most is that a man had just come back to where we lived in Saigon. He had all this beard, and he looked kind of unclean, and he grabbed me and kissed me. I said, "Who is this man?" When my mom came out and started hugging him, I said, "Who is this?" Finally, she told me that he was my dad. I said: "It's my dad? I've never seen him before." Because he had served in the South Vietnamese Army, he had been in a reeducation camp ever since I was born.

When my dad came back from the reeducation camp, he did not have a job, so my mom had to work very hard selling vegetables in the open market. She had to wake up at 5:00 in the morning and didn't come home till 7:00 or 8:00 at night. I did not get the chance to see her until late in the evening when we ate dinner together.

As a child in post–1975 Vietnam, I particularly disliked one thing. To enter school every day, you had to wear a red handkerchief that stood for your loyalty to the Communist government. If you didn't wear it, you couldn't go to school. None of us wanted to wear the red handkerchief, and we often asked each other, "What is this for?" But we had to wear it.

Duyen, Long, Lan, and Linh Nguyen in Saigon, about 1985.

Some would just put it on their neck to get into the school, and once they were in, they would take it off. Whenever they saw a teacher, they put it back on. We all made fun of it.

Most of the time my maternal grandma took care of us and all the rest of her grandkids. She had a lot of children and lived with my family near all of my relatives. She got up at 5:00 in the morning and cooked some food for my grandpa. After that she went to the house of one of her other daughters and took care of the kids there. Then she would go to another aunt's house. She would spend the whole day going to different houses to take care of her grandchildren. Finally, she would come back to my house and take care of us and cook. My grandma is the best.

We lived like that for a while until my dad said, "We've got to leave this country because if we stay here, we will have nothing." We worked very hard just to get enough food. But no matter how hard a person worked, it wasn't always possible to get an education in Vietnam, especially if your father had served with the Americans. Most people just went to school through the sixth or seventh grade, just enough to learn to read and write a little and do simple math. It was especially hard to get from the ninth grade to the tenth. You had to take a very difficult test. Even if you passed the test, it was still extremely difficult to get from the twelfth grade to college. You either had to be a child of the V.C. [Viet Cong] to get in, or you had to be extremely smart. But even if you got in college, studied hard, and graduated, you might still wind up sitting on the street selling cologne, cigarettes, and vegetables forever.

So you see there was nothing really to hold us there. The government was corrupt. For example, if the local policemen knew that your family had served in the South Vietnamese government, they would keep looking at your house as if it had a lot of money in it. If they knew you had money, you had to bribe them to leave you alone. Under such conditions there was no promise for the future. So my parents decided to leave the country.

First, my dad and my second sister, Dung, left the country together. They had to try several times before they successfully got out in 1983. Then they stayed near Kuala Lumpur in Malaysia for several years before they were accepted into America. When my oldest sister, Linh, was about 12, she tried to escape with my aunt. When Linh got caught, the Communists put her in jail for several months with my aunt and my cousin. Linh was put in prison several times, but she eventually escaped to Malaysia and then to the United States.

In 1987 when my mom, my little brother, and I left Saigon, I didn't

even know we were trying to escape. I just knew that we were going somewhere. That day my grandma woke me up at about 5:00 in the morning,
and she was packing clothes for me. My brother was crying because he
wanted some milk. He was only about three or four years old. I was about
eleven. I can't remember exactly because age is not very important in Vietnam. I don't even know my birthday. My parents can't remember any of
our birthdays because it was not considered important there. While I don't
know my exact age when we left, I do know that we came to the United
States in 1987. We must have escaped in January or February of 1987
because I stayed in a Thai camp only six months, and I know we left after
the Vietnamese New Year.

Anyway, my mom was trying to pack my brother's clothes and keep
him quiet so we could leave without drawing the neighbors' attention. But
we had already tried twice and hadn't gotten out of the country yet. This
was the third try, and this time we were successful.

Our plan was to escape from Vietnam to Cambodia and then escape
from Cambodia to Thailand. Part of the way across Vietnam, from Saigon
to Tan Chau just east of the Cambodian border, we had to go by bus.
There were no seats left on the bus, so we sat in the aisle, where it was
very crowded. After that we had to switch to a public van, where about
15 people were crowded together. For those three hours we could hardly
breathe. After that, we rode a motorcycle. I got to ride on the same motorcycle with my mother and my little brother.

During the escape my other two cousins, Dien Le and Huong
Nguyen, also went with my mom, my brother, and me. We rode two
motorcycles to Phnom Penh, Cambodia, and stayed there for a few days.
The people who were helping us didn't let us go out of the house because
they were afraid that other people would see us and say we weren't from
Cambodia. After a few days, other people on motorcycles came and picked
us up. They said they were going to drive us to a big boat, a freighter. However, the unlucky thing was that the people leading us on motorcycles
went to the wrong port, so we didn't get on the boat.

Instead, we had to go back into inland Cambodia. We said, "Well, if
we can't get on the big boat, we have to think up another way to get into
Thailand." We stayed in Cambodia for another week, and suddenly our
helpers said, "Now is the time to go." We got on the motorcycles, and they
drove us to the place where policemen lived. We were scared, thinking,
"Oh, my gosh, are they going to turn us in?" These people could have
betrayed us easily. But as it turned out, the policemen took a bribe to let
us stay there for a few days, and then a few days later they showed us the
way to get out to the beach. We had to walk in the jungle for a few hours

without water. When we got to a small pond in the jungle, we were afraid of drinking the water because there were mosquitoes, and we were afraid of malaria. But we had to drink the water anyway because we were thirsty. Then we walked some more until we arrived at the beach, where we got into a very small boat. The group escaping was my mom, my brother, my two cousins, me, and three other people. The fishing boat was extremely small, and even though I was small I had to squat down under the deck. I was hungry and thirsty. I said, "Mommy, Mommy, I'm thirsty." Before escaping, she had prepared everything—water, food, everything. But the helpers had said: "Oh, you don't need this. You are going to be on a big boat." So the only thing she had was a few bags of dried noodles. I didn't want to eat it, but she said, "You have to eat it," and I put some in my mouth.

We rode in the boat overnight. When I woke up in the morning, the fishermen said: "We've gotten to the place where we are going. Now you have to get off." When the fishermen stopped at this wilderness spot, they were going to drop us off in the water—not directly on the shore. Because I was small, my feet didn't touch the bottom. My mother was begging the fisherman to please put me on his shoulders and walk me to the shore because she was too weak. One of my cousins was holding my brother, and my other cousin was unable to help me. So one of the fishermen put me on his shoulders, but he didn't walk me all the way to the shore. He dropped me in the water and said, "Here, this is good enough." But I couldn't feel the bottom with my feet. Although I thought I was drowning, I didn't lose my head. I swirled around and was finally able to grab a branch and pull myself up. I thought I was so lucky. I didn't even tell my mother how scared I was because my brother was crying and hungry. Even now I don't try to swim because of that experience.

Although we were technically in Thailand, the place where we were dropped off was still about two miles from a safe Thai port. Sharp, slippery rocks lined the shore, and beyond the rocky shore was the thick jungle. If we went up there, we might get lost.

So when we all got on shore, we tried to get the attention of the Thai navy. There were small Thai boats that sailed in and out, but they didn't get too close to the shore because the waves would push the boats in and crush them. The boats were too far away, and we were just a few people who couldn't get their attention. We waved and yelled at them for about three hours. Everybody was hungry and thirsty, especially my brother, who kept crying and crying. My mom didn't know what to do, and we all thought we were going to die of thirst and hunger. Finally my cousin said that if all of us couldn't go up the shore to the port, then he and another guy would walk through the jungle together. Then they left us and walked straight into the jungle to find help.

After being gone for more than two hours, my cousin came back with others to help us, but they couldn't speak Vietnamese. Eventually they sent a small boat and tried to get us all in the boat. At the time, the waves were very big, making it hard to get in. They said at first they were just going to put us small kids in and come back for the older people later, but then they decided to put us all in. Soon they got us to the safe port, where they gave us food and drink. When my brother saw food and water, he drank and ate and ate. An hour later he vomited because he was too tired and had eaten too much. Everybody laughed at him. We were so happy to be rescued.

My mom showed those who had helped us a gold ring that she had knit into my clothes. Because they saved us, she offered them the ring. They refused to take it, and she was surprised because she had heard that often foreigners who help escapees would take gold by force. But these people were in the military and their captain said they couldn't accept gifts, so they didn't. These people said they were going to take us to the camp the next day, and they offered us water from a well to take a shower, but we didn't shower because the water was so dirty. That night we slept on the dock. Even though we had nothing to sleep on or put over us, and we were cold, we were still safe and happy because they were going to let us into a camp.

The next morning we got into a big boat and went down a river until they stopped and told us we would have to walk about a mile or so to the small temporary camp. Because it was very hot that day and we didn't have any shoes on, we had to walk on tiptoes down the concrete road.

When we got to the Thai camp, there were many Vietnamese people. After the camp officials wrote our names down, they gave us a small space to stay in. However, our space was near the smelly sewer. We didn't have anything—no blankets or anything else. My mother took out a gold ring because she had heard that a Thai man in camp would go into town and convert goods into money. He kept one-third or more of the value for himself. But we needed money to buy clothes because those who ran the camp didn't provide anything. When the man came back with the money, my mom bought some blankets, and the next day she got some pots and pans and some rice. The camp provided us with a little bit of food, but not much.

The people who guarded the temporary camp were horrible. The guards were sometimes rapists. If they saw a young girl and they wanted to make her sleep with them, they might beat her if she resisted. My mother was worried for my cousin Huong, who was about 16 or 17 then, and Mom would tell my male cousins to watch out for her. Mom was also careful about our sleeping arrangements, always putting my female cousin in the middle.

I remember an incident involving two men who were our friends in this camp. They were half-Vietnamese and half-Chinese. One day an official, a man who did paperwork, asked them to carry some things to a truck. They agreed to help him, but when they returned, the guards were very angry. The guards yelled at the two men and asked who had given them permission to leave. Our friends tried to explain that the official had asked them to accompany him to load the truck, but the guards beat them and kicked them with their boots. Their faces were all bruised and swollen, and my mother tried to treat them to make their wounds better.

The guards treated us badly. Every morning we had to stand in line. They would call each person's name out, and then sometimes they would call out a young girl to sing for them. They would even call my cousin out and make her sing. She was scared and shy. My mother would tell her to sing any song so they wouldn't beat her up. They liked to make fun of people. If there was somebody they didn't like—man, woman, old, young, whatever—they would call them out and talk about them and make fun of them. Every time I remember that camp, it upsets me because they didn't treat us like humans.

Despite this treatment, I didn't regret leaving Vietnam. My mom also didn't seem to regret leaving Vietnam. We tried to keep in mind that life in this camp was a temporary arrangement. We would hang on, and later things would be better. We had escaped, and we couldn't go back. We had to keep on every day.

During the month we lived in the temporary camp, our assigned space had a roof, but there were no complete walls. It wasn't like a house. We were lucky it didn't rain much. It was very open, but there was shelter.

To find out when we could move to the Thai permanent camp, we had to keep checking with the camp office every day. We just had to sit there and wait. I think we got to leave within a month because of the incident with the guards who beat up the two men. That event made the man who did paperwork very angry. When he reported the incident to higher officials, the guards were scared. They got punished and sent away. At the same time the camp officials shipped a lot of people to the permanent camp, including us. They put us all in a big military truck and drove us to the permanent camp.

We got to the outskirts of the permanent camp at Phanat Nikhom within a few hours. But we couldn't go inside the camp yet. They called our names and divided us into sections, and then we walked into the permanent camp. My sister Duyen was already there, but we didn't know that yet.

Duyen had escaped Vietnam a month earlier than we did. All we knew was that she had escaped to Thailand, but we didn't know which camp she was in. My mother was worried and hoping Duyen was in this camp. Later Duyen told me that during the time that we were walking through the camp, she heard on the intercom that there were new people arriving, and she was excited and hopeful. She said every time she heard there were new people, she would run to the gate and check to see if we had come because my mom had told her before she escaped: "Go with your cousin. We will be right behind." Even though Duyen checked every time she heard that new people had come to the camp, she missed us the day we arrived.

The Phanat Nikhom camp officials showed us our place to stay. The camp was divided into sections and our section was next to where my cousin who had escaped with Duyen was staying. Duyen was in a place called the minors' area, where people who were under 18 and without parents were placed. Many volunteers from America and Australia were there to take care of the minors, as well as a sister from some church. Because of these people, the minors' treatment was special.

We stayed in a big building that wasn't divided into rooms but into sleeping spaces. You could try to put up a bamboo curtain if you had the money to buy one, but there was no privacy. If you wanted to say something, your neighbor could hear you. There was no door.

The bathroom was a nightmare. You squatted over it and then poured water into it when you were done. Because it didn't operate properly, I avoided it as much as possible. The smell was awful, and it was near where everybody lived. I always think about that when I think of the permanent camp.

We stayed in the permanent camp near Phanat Nikhom for about six months. My mom, my brother, and I were together; my male cousin Dien stayed with us because my mom wanted him to protect us. My girl cousin Huong was next door with my other cousin who had come in first with Duyen. They stayed there together so they would feel safe. I don't know why this girl cousin wasn't in the minors' section because she was under 18 and without parents. Whether they put her in there or not was all a matter of paperwork.

Eventually my mother found out, from a cousin, that Duyen was in the minors' section. He told Duyen where we were, and she came right over to see us. She and my mom talked until late, but she had to be back in the minors' section by the 9:00 P.M. curfew. My mom wanted Duyen to stay in the minors' section because it was better for her, and she could visit us freely in the daytime.

This camp was much bigger than the temporary camp. They had a place for kids to play, a market, restaurants, and a movie. They had lots of things to do, but to go to these places, you had to have money, and they didn't provide us with money. They just gave us food: rice and meat and vegetables. They would give us just a small piece of chicken for four people for three days, so whatever gold rings we still had left, my mom had to use up. She wrote a letter to my dad, who was already in Memphis and working in maintenance at an airport. She asked him to send some money. She also wrote my aunts in Memphis and asked them to send money.

My father and aunts weren't able to send a lot of money because they were living on food stamps and making very little money. But they sent a little, and it was helpful because a dollar in the camp could go a long way. One dollar here would be worth ten baht there [Thailand]. So I did get to see some movies, since a children's ticket cost only three baht. I also got to know some people in the theater, some men who had been South Vietnamese soldiers and who liked to have kids around. They felt as if they were protecting us. They probably missed their families because they treated us like brothers and sisters. Sometimes they would let us see the movies for free. The movies were Chinese and dubbed in Thai. But there were some Vietnamese people who had been there long enough to learn Thai, and they would translate the movie into Vietnamese for the audience over a microphone. Some of their translation wasn't exact because when I got to America, I would discuss these movies with my sisters or cousins, and we realized that we had heard different translations.

Compared with life in the temporary camp, our life in the permanent camp was wonderful because we were able to have some money from my father and my aunts and uncles in Memphis. We could buy extra food to eat and clothes to wear. Compared with the other people in the camp, we were much better off because most of them didn't have relatives in America. They lived day by day on whatever food they were given.

Since we were only a small woman and some children, it was hard for us to carry the heavy water back to our section. So we would hire the young men to carry water for us. Also, some men worked by providing protection to others. We lived next to two men who had been there a long time, and they were in charge of the section we were in. My mom gave them money and told them to watch over us.

At this camp, people were not publicly beaten. But the main guard was mean, and whoever broke the law was put in prison, especially men.

Sometimes the guards shaved the prisoners' heads to shame them, and beat them up. But it was more often because some people broke the camp rules, and that wasn't too bad. One rule we had to obey involved the Thai national anthem. Every morning when we heard it played, we had to stand still and bow our heads, unless we were in the house.

I went to two different schools in the camp. One class, from 1:00 to 4:00 P.M., was like a Vietnamese school that taught regular subjects such as the Vietnamese language, science, math, and social studies. But I also went to morning classes for adults because I wanted to learn English. At age 11, I was the youngest in the class and received attention for doing so well, but it is easier for young people to learn a foreign language. These classes lasted two to three hours, five days a week. Because the man who taught us was Vietnamese, some of the pronunciation was not correct. I am still trying to correct some mistakes that are firmly imprinted in my brain because that was the first time I learned English and I studied it this way for six months.

At Phanat Nikhom they had a campwide intercom. Every day they wanted to interview certain persons, so you had to listen carefully to the intercom. When your name was called, you would go to the office to be interviewed. My mom stayed in the house every day and listened to the intercom. If she heard our name, she would call us home, and we would go for an interview. Sometimes if they called your name and you didn't go right away, they would say to come the next day, or two days later, or three days. They would call you about three times a day to be sure you didn't miss your name.

We waited a long time to be called for our first interview. But after we had all had a first interview, there was a much shorter time before we were called again. The sooner you could get through an interview, the better.

When they called us to interview, our whole family went, including my mom, my sister, my brother, and me. The interviewer was an American, but we had a Vietnamese translator who lived in the camp and worked for the Americans. The interview usually took an hour or two. Before my mom left Vietnam, she had used permanent ink to write down my dad's address in Memphis on two pockets of the jeans I wore. I had another pair of jeans, and she wrote it in the pocket of those too. I always had to wear those jeans. Even if I lost everything else, I would still have my father's name and his American address. Also, my mom sewed gold rings into our clothes. So everything we wore was important to us.

Meanwhile, my dad was in Memphis doing some kind of paperwork to get us over there, saying that his wife and kids were staying in this camp and these were their names. We were trying to get the two sets of paperwork connected so that we could get to the United States. My family was very lucky because it consisted of a husband and wife, four daughters, and our little brother. The Thai officials put a higher priority on getting parents, young children, and pregnant women out than on people who were more than 18 years old and without a family. That's how we were able to leave the Thai permanent camp so quickly, after only six months. Another advantage was that my dad knew someone in the United States who dealt with immigration paperwork.

Two weeks after our second interview, they called us again and told us we each had to have medical exams. Then we knew for sure that we were leaving because they always have you checked by a doctor before you leave. The forms the doctor filled out completed our paperwork. After the exams, the camp officials told us we would be leaving in the next week and that we must be ready to go.

When I found out that I was actually going to the United States, I thought: "Oh, wow. I'm going to America." Everything entered my mind: Oh, America—no dirt on the streets. I imagined some perfect place where everything is clean and our house is nice. Because we had been living around so much dirt, the first thing that entered my mind was a clean place with a lot of light and beautiful buildings. I was very glad to leave the camp because people said that America was wonderful. I almost imagined a utopia.

The day we left, we got on a van and were driven into Bangkok to Don Muang Airport. It was our first time to see an airport. They had an automatic elevator. We were all going, "Wow." We were amazed at the sights. Also, I didn't realize that the wall in the airport was glass, and I tried to walk through it. It was a good day for me because I got to see many new things and many people from different countries speaking different languages. When we finally got on the airplane, we were scared and amazed at the same time. When they told us to put on our seatbelts, we didn't understand, but we looked around and saw what others were doing and did that too.

Although I became a U.S. citizen when I was a freshman at Christian Brothers University in Memphis, someday I would like to go back and visit Vietnam because it is still my country. My grandparents are there, and I want to go back and see my grandma who took care of us. She is in her late eighties now and has Alzheimer's. We have hired two people to take care of her. She lives with my grandfather, but she doesn't know anybody, and she can't take care of herself or even feed herself. Somebody has to put food in her mouth, and if nobody watches her, she wanders off.

It's too bad that when she has grandkids to send her money and take good care of her, she can't enjoy it. She doesn't even know about it. When we escaped from Vietnam, I could see that she was very sad that we were going to leave her. All of her children are in Memphis, so there are no kids there to take care of her. I don't say I could ever repay what she did for us, but I am sorry that she can't see her grandkids, can't see how well we have done and be proud of us so that she could say, "Wow, those are my grandkids!" Now she doesn't know anything. When my second sister, Dung, and my mother went back to Vietnam during Christmas 1995, Dung said my grandma couldn't recognize her or my mom. Today a picture of my grandmother hangs in our den in Memphis. It shows a woman with short hair and black teeth from chewing cau trau. She is a very warm, caring person whom we love dearly.

That Christmas 1995 trip was my mom's second trip back to Vietnam since our escape. My dad hasn't been back yet because he doesn't want to see the V.C. [Viet Cong] and also because he wants to save up a lot of money first. All of his relatives are still there, and when he goes back, he wants to have plenty of money for their support. Because my mother's people are all here except her parents, she can go back more often because she needs to take care only of my grandparents and maybe a couple of second cousins. I don't think she wanted to stay in Vietnam after either visit. Everything is so much cleaner here. When she went back to Vietnam, everything was dirty, and noisy, and too hot, and people's attitudes were intimidating. In America, people don't have to be tough and fight the way they do in Vietnam. You just go to work and come home and cook. You don't have to fight.

The attitudes of people in Vietnam are different to Mom now, and she doesn't think she could blend back into that style of living. I didn't think she wanted to stay there. Of course, she wanted to stay there longer with my grandparents, but not to live there.

My dad says that when he goes back, he would like to live there, but in the countryside. He would want to retire and go fishing in the country.

Chapter 5

If I Die, Will
Anybody Know?

Duyen Nguyen graduated in 1996 from Christian Brothers
University with a major in biology and went on to study at
the West Virginia Osteopathic Medical School in Lewisburg.
Duyen worked for a year as a research technician at St. Jude
Children's Research Hospital. She enjoys swimming, tennis,
in-line skating, and racquetball.

When the Communists took over my country in 1975, my father was put
in prison for six years for what was called "reeducation." But it was not
reeducation. The Communists just wanted to torture those people who
had worked for the American government. They made my father work
very hard and punished him for his American connections. While he was
in prison, my mother was the only one to support the four girls in the family. A year after my father returned to Saigon, my mother became pregnant with my brother, my parents' fifth and last child.

My father had been back with us for only two years when my family
decided to escape from Vietnam. It was very hard to survive in our country after the Communists took over because we didn't have the freedom
to do anything. We didn't have the freedom to speak or to vote. What our
parents wanted most was for us to have the opportunity in the United
States for better lives and better educations.

In 1983 my father and my second-oldest sister, Dung, were the first
ones in our family to escape from Vietnam. They spent a couple of years
in a Malaysian refugee camp. Then my uncle in Memphis sponsored them,

and they came to Memphis. Two or three years later, my older sister Linh escaped with my aunt. And then in 1987, when I was about 13, I escaped without any of my immediate family members.

My mom made secret arrangements with some people and paid them to help me escape. When I escaped, I went with my second cousin Duc. I didn't know him before because he was from Da Nang. He came to Saigon to spend a couple of months with us and to escape with me.

The night before the escape, I was staying at my grandmom's house, something I often did. In the morning while it was still dark, my cousin told me to get on a bicycle with him, and we rode to the bus station. I took a bag with some clothes, and I also had a gold ring that my mom had sewn inside my shirt. We caught a bus and went somewhere southwest of Saigon. Before we reached Cambodia, we switched to a van. We had to ride on the luggage rack on top of this van with a lot of Cambodians. It was very scary because the road was bad, and I was afraid I would fall. When we crossed the border, Cambodian soldiers checked to see if we were Cambodian or not. My cousin Duc and I were in a panic because if they recognized that we were Vietnamese, they could put us in prison. Luckily, we passed through, and they didn't ask us anything.

When we got farther into Cambodia, we got on a motorcycle that another guy drove. This guy drove up hills and down hills. We were on the motorcycle for eight hours, from daylight until dark, with dirt always getting on our faces. I was very tired.

Finally, we came to the house of a Cambodian lady. I don't know who she was—probably some contact person. We stayed inside her house for four or five days. We couldn't go out anywhere because we might be recognized as Vietnamese.

In her house I was thinking: "Wow, what's going on? I should be in the United States by now." I got really excited about leaving her house because I thought that when I got out, I would go to the United States immediately. I didn't know I had to go through many more things first. When I realized that we had to stay in this lady's house for several days, I started crying. I cried and asked Duc: "Why are we staying here? I want to go to the United States because my daddy is there, and I want to see him." But my cousin told me that we had to stay there for a while.

In the middle of the fifth night, the lady told us to leave the house and follow her. She took us to a small, very dark house in the forest. There was a group of people moving around. Somehow, the lady forgot to bring my bag of clothes. She said she would bring it to me, but she didn't. So I had nothing with me, only some medication for seasickness. We were in the little house for about half an hour. Then they led us a short distance

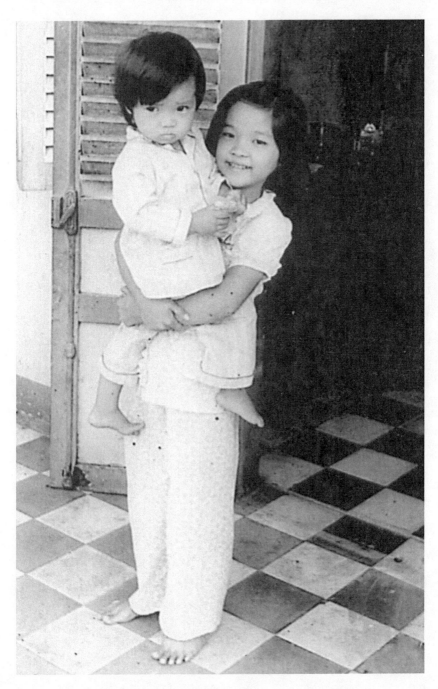

Duyen Nguyen holding her brother, Long, in Saigon, 1985.

to a small boat. About 20 of us got into the boat. I didn't know who the other people were, and it was very dark in the boat. I was wondering where I was and where they were taking me. Then I thought: "Oh, my God, what if I die on the ocean? Would anybody know?" Before, in Vietnam, I had heard stories about people who escaped but could not survive on the ocean because they ran out of gas or ran out of food. So I just sat there and kept crying and crying.

The most adventurous part of the boat trip was when we crossed the marine border between Cambodia and Thailand. The man who had been hired to take us was very nervous because of the people on the sea who check you out—like the coast guard or the navy. We were all nervously hiding under the deck. A few hours later I heard him say: "We made it. We've crossed the marine border, and we're safe now." The next morning we reached the Thai coast. Our boat trip had taken only one night.

Early in the morning the man running the boat dropped us on some rocks very close to the land. He and his men just left us there. After we climbed on the rocks to the shore, we came to a forest. Two of the young men in our group decided to cross the forest to find somebody to help us. We were scared. We wondered if these two guys would get captured or eaten by tigers. Then what would we do? But we knew this was the only thing to do. They had to risk going into the forest, or we'd all be stuck there. After about an hour, they came back with a few Thai soldiers. We were so happy they had made it.

However, these Thai soldiers were very rude. They tried to rob us. They told us that anyone who had money or jewelry had to give it to them. We had no choice but to do it because we needed their assistance. But they didn't get my gold ring sewn into my shirt. Other people wearing gold on their hands or necks had to give it to the soldiers. Then they took us to a small camp and let us eat some rice. When they gave us the rice, we asked for chopsticks, but they didn't have any. We had to use our hands. We stayed there for a few hours while they contacted some people to take us to a bigger camp.

A few hours later they took us in a truck to this larger place. It was still not the main camp, only a temporary one. While we were there, they let us 20 people stay together. They gave us only a small amount to eat each day, and our water was from the lake nearby. It was horrible. I looked at the water and said, "Oh, I have to take a bath and drink from this?" But we had no choice. I was crying every day while we were there. I was asking my cousin Duc: "Why are we staying here? Can't we go somewhere better?" And he would remind me to be patient because we only were there temporarily.

Duyen Nguyen (front row right) with her family in Saigon, about 1985: sisters Linh (back row right) and Lan (front row center); cousin Hoa Le (front row left); brother Long (in mother's arms); and mother Thuy.

We stayed there for three weeks before being transferred to the main camp. At this camp, they wouldn't let me stay with my cousin. They split us up because they categorized me as a minor. My cousin was just my second cousin, not like a brother, so I could not stay with him. Once again I cried because I had to go a different way from my cousin. They took me to a minors' center, where all the children lived who came without their parents.

At first I couldn't get used to it, and I cried because I didn't know anybody. But then later I felt better because the minors' center was run by Catholic sisters and brothers. They were the ones who taught us and took care of us. After a few days, I felt better and made more friends because the kids were in the same situation that I was in. The kids were from all over Vietnam and were all different ages. Some who were only five or six years old had come with their older brothers or sisters.

We had activities every day. For example, we would go to class every day to study math, English, and some other subjects. We would also play soccer, even though we didn't have any tennis shoes. We had to play with our bare feet, since we could not run with sandals. Even though it hurt my feet, I enjoyed it. We also were divided into teams to distribute the water. Every day a different group would get to distribute water to the rest of the kids. So we had lots of fun playing and fighting with the water. When the rains came, we would be happy because we could have some more water. Then we would all run out and get the bucket, catch the rain in it, and just lie down under the pouring sky.

In some ways, I think that was the best time of my childhood. Although I spent only seven months there, I made so many friends, both boys and girls. After ten years I am still in contact with four of them. Before I left, I gave them my father's Memphis address and phone number. After I came to the United States, I wrote them letters at the camp. Two or three years later, they all came to the United States, and we still keep in touch. Sometimes we talk on the phone, and sometimes we e-mail each other. One is in Virginia, another is in Connecticut, and two are in California.

After being in the minors' center for two or three weeks, I learned that my mom had come to the camp. My mom, my little brother, Long, and my younger sister, Lan, had escaped two or three weeks after me and had come along the same road. My mom told me that she had been through more difficulties than I had. Although I didn't realize it at the time, my trip had been almost perfect. I was so happy that Mom had come that I cried when I finally saw her. I couldn't believe that I was seeing her again so soon.

After my mom, brother, and sister came, I still lived in the minors' center because the conditions were better. I decided to stay there and get to know more friends and learn more. Besides, I could still go out and eat with my mother.

My family was in a better situation than many other people because we had my father in Memphis, and he sent us some money. Overall, we had enough food to eat and lived better than other people who didn't have any relatives in the United States. We were very lucky because we stayed only about seven months in the refugee camp and were able to come to the United States together.

When the time came for us to leave Thailand, camp personnel took us from the camp by bus to the Bangkok airport. I had never seen an airport before. I was saying: "This is the airport? Where are we going?" On the airplane they gave us American food to eat, but I could not eat any of it, not even the orange juice. I had never tasted orange juice before, and it seemed bitter to me. Then they gave us Coke, and I had never had Coke either. It had too much gas. It made me burp and made my nose feel weird. I also got airsick and threw up. It took too long—almost a whole day—to get to the United States. I kept asking myself, "When will we get there?" It was so tiring to sit there and not move or do anything for almost 24 hours. After switching to another plane in Tokyo, we went to California, where we missed the plane for Memphis. After we had waited for several hours, a man came up and told us that we were going to a motel to spend the night. That ride from the airport to the motel was the first time I saw America. We rode in a car. I looked at the car and thought it was so beautiful. Everything I saw in America looked totally different and strange to me. He took us to the motel, where I took a shower. I didn't know which handle was for hot water and which was for cold, and when I put my hand under the faucet, I screamed because it was too hot.

After we got settled into the motel, we called my father and let him know we were in California. The next morning when we arrived in Memphis, there were so many people at the airport. A lot of my relatives had come here before us, and my father now had lots of friends. When I got out of the airplane and saw all these people, I could not remember who was who. All my cousins had changed. Everything looked strange. But I was happy that my family could be united after five years of being separated.

Chapter 6
Our Lady of the Boat

Ha Nguyen graduated from the University of Memphis in
May 1997 with a major in biology and went on to study at the
Southern College of Optometry in Memphis.

One of the main reasons my family wanted to leave Vietnam was because
we didn't have much freedom in our country. Government officials often
came to our house to find out who was home. People did not have the right
to do as many things as you do over here. For example, if you had money,
opened a store, and began making a profit, a government official could suddenly take over your store. You could lose all the money and all the effort
you had put into it. This is what the Communists did when they took over
South Vietnam in 1975; that's what they did to almost everybody. Rich
people, prosperous people—all became poor, and a lot of them left the country. Of course, there were people who were able to keep their money because
they hid it. If they didn't hide it, they would have lost almost everything. It
became very discouraging to everyone. Many people wanted to open a business in Vietnam but were afraid to because the government would take it.
There is no point in starting something if you can't get anything out of it.

Also, if a policeman didn't like you, he could just make up a reason
and take you to jail. If the government officials suspected you of a crime,
they could put you in jail and beat you until you accepted responsibility
for the crime. They don't give you a fair trial. In the United States if you
can't afford a lawyer, the government will provide one. I've never heard of
anything like that in my country. Once the police thought a lady who lived
next door to us knew something about a theft. They beat her even though
she was pregnant, and she lost the child. She didn't know anything, but

there was nothing anyone could do to stop the police. These are some of the reasons my people would get discouraged and want to go away.

Before the war, there was a lot of freedom, much as there is over here. There were modern things, like refrigerators. The lifestyle was better. There was more opportunity. The government was more fair.

My father used to work in Saigon for the former government, so when the Communists took over, they didn't look very favorably on him. If I wanted to go to medical school, for instance, my chances were very slim, even if I did very well in school, because of my father's background. They might not even allow me to turn in an application. Opportunities were very limited. You had to do extremely well in high school to get into college. A lot of people dropped out of high school because they needed to help support their families and could not afford to study. To get away from these conditions, my parents considered escaping during 1975 even while the war was still going on. However, they were not sure what it was like in America. After a while, however, some of my cousins and uncles came over here. They found it friendly, and they liked it, so we felt safe enough to take the chance to come here. Even with the Orderly Departure Program in place then, it was still very difficult to get out. So my parents felt they didn't have any choice but to escape. When they finally decided to go, my parents contacted someone who arranged for people to leave the country. They paid this person ahead of time. He let us know only a few days before it was time to leave. He said where to go, and we went.

That morning in April 1985 my mom, my two sisters, my younger brother, and I left the house in Saigon. I was ten years old. At first we walked as if we were going to the zoo. But then we got in a van and a man started driving us around town. The van twisted and turned around Saigon until it was night. Finally, we arrived near a group of trees, where it was very dark and muddy. I had fallen asleep, so I didn't know what was going on. Suddenly people were yelling: "Get off the van! Get off the van!" The place was so dirty, so muddy. We went down a hill and climbed aboard a small shallow boat, something like a canoe, and some people rowed us out to a fishing boat in deeper water. Once on the fishing boat, we were told to hide below the deck. After the boat left, it had to pass through several inspection stations.

Meanwhile, under the deck it was really dark. Also, there wasn't much air below because about 50 people were huddled together. I needed some air because so many people were crammed in, and some were urinating. I felt like vomiting. The people on the deck were just trying to take care of everybody by getting past the inspection stations, so there wasn't much concern for what was going on down below. Some people fainted. Then I fell asleep because it was so hot. Later in the evening when we got past all the inspection stations, someone started cooking a watery rice soup. It felt so comforting and so good after being hungry all day. They also made some lemonade that helped us feel better after our exhausting day.

We spent that whole night under the deck. The next morning they told us it was safe, and we started coming up on top. It was good to see the light, breathe fresh air, and have more space to move.

I didn't know what the next day would be like. Those days I was so scared. Even when it was daylight and we were on deck, I was still scared. We were on the ocean for three days, and nobody rescued us.

Once we saw a large boat, but they made no move to rescue us. We were scared because we were running out of food. At first we had enough to last for three days. We also had fish from the ocean, and some fish stored in an icebox. I don't know if those in charge expected us to be rescued in three days, but the food dwindled.

The waves kept going up and down, up and down. One day the wind blew very hard, and it was raining. I didn't know how to swim, and I was afraid of the water. I'm sure the other kids were scared too.

On nights when we had high winds and rain, I couldn't sleep. I might fall asleep, but then I'd wake up. When no boats rescued us, people started getting panicky. It seemed like things were getting out of order. Fortunately, we met two small fishing boats from Indonesia. These people agreed to row us to a small island if we paid them, but no one had any money. Then a doctor on our boat agreed to give up his valuable watch, and the men on the two boats helped us in exchange for the watch. We were all thankful. We needed these men as navigators because they claimed they knew the area. There were lots of rocks on the way to the island, and if you were not careful, your boat would break up. We had heard of people who had died that way. We switched to the two boats, and the fishermen rowed us to Lang Da, an island so small you could see the whole thing. As we headed for the island, it began to rain hard. Water was getting into the boat, and people were bailing it out. I had heard a story about people on one boat: they saw the little island, and they were so happy that they started going toward it too quickly. They got almost to it, and the boat broke up on the rocks. Everyone died but one person. This man went crazy because all his family had died and he was the only survivor.

When we got to the island, we met a family who had a big house, so big all of us could fit in it. We stayed in their huge combined living room and dining room, and they gave us crackers to eat. They were private citizens, and it was their home. They seemed so nice. They let us use their bathrooms and let us sleep. The next morning they told us to come into another room one by one, and they started searching us for gold. When one man in our group had a gold chain that he did not want to give up, I saw an Indonesian man point a gun at him.

The next day we got on a bigger old boat that took us to another Indonesian island called Tam Pa. This was also a small island, but larger than the first. Again all 50 of us lived in one house. It was large, long, and very dark inside, with only one lightbulb. Also, it was extremely hot.

Every day we were given a small allotment of rice. The rice was not enough for everyone. We were also given soy sauce, but it had a sandy taste. We ate as much food as we could while also leaving some for others. We did our best to get along with each other because we were all trying to survive. Sometimes there was a little arguing, but most of the time it was all right. We lived there for a few days.

After we left Tam Pa, we went to another island I would pronounce "KuKu." We lived there for a month or so. On this island they treated us much better. We lived in a house that was neither brick nor wood. It was something that could stay on sand because the floor of the house was sand. In front of the house was the beach. The people gave us good white rice and sometimes fish. If people didn't use all their allotment of rice, they could exchange it with the fishermen for fish. Occasionally some of the Indonesian men would give candy to the children. There were papaya trees and shells on the shore to play with. We could swim in the ocean.

I remember one incident, though, about a man who stole a fish. When the Indonesian officials found out about it, they beat him so much his nose started bleeding. I was scared and thought those people were cruel, but I guess their behavior depended on who was guilty of what. It was an incident that made me know I had to behave correctly.

We lived on Kuku for a month, then moved to Pulau Galang, where we stayed for a year and a half. Again all 50 people lived in the same house. Although this was a small house, it was made of wood and was much better than the one before. We slept on a bench that stretched from one side of the room to the other. It was not soft, but it was off the floor, and it was comforting. In our country we sleep on a wooden bed, so it was similar and that was all right.

The Indonesians gave us rice, some eggs (according to your family size), flour, sugar, and green beans. Some people even grew vegetables. You could get fresh drinking water from the camp officials. We caught rainwater for washing in containers. But normally, when we would take a bath, we would take it in a spring. The spring water was yellow, but it felt good because it was hot on our island and the water was cool. Everyone would just jump in and take a bath. It seemed normal then.

If we didn't eat all the things they had given us, we could sell them, get a little money, and buy one thing, such as a chicken. One time my mom bought a chicken, and it was a wonderful thing. The chicken there isn't like the chicken here. Instead of being soft, it's more elastic. It's like chewing gum; you have to chew it really hard. When we had something special, like the chicken, we usually shared.

At Galang there were many people who came from other boats, but we didn't know them. Even though it was one island, it had two separate refugee areas called Galang I and Galang II. That island was quite entertaining because there was a cafe, a fruit market, and a supermarket where they sold different things like candy. I also knew there was a theater on the island. My sister went, but the movie she saw was about a snake-girl, and I was so scared that I didn't go.

Newcomers came to Galang I. The lifestyle I just described to you is that of Galang I. At Galang I, there was also a school where they taught English to adults only. Children did not have English classes but were taught other subjects in Vietnamese. I took a math class and a biology class, and I was also able to sit in on my father's English class. There was also a language room where he could listen to English tapes. When you had lived at Galang I for a while and your papers looked acceptable, you could move to a higher level and had a greater chance of going to America. Then you moved to Galang II. When we moved to Galang II, our family had a house all to ourselves, not with 50 people as before in Galang I. I felt very good about that. We had more privacy. We had a restroom, and we would sleep upstairs and cook downstairs. There was a hammock that someone put up, and I remember I would lie in the hammock in the afternoon and read novels and fall asleep. That was what I had done back in my country, and that is what I did in Galang II. I guess my father put it up because he knew I loved doing that. Galang II was windy because we lived high on a hill and so was not as hot as Galang I.

Whenever it would rain in Galang I, we would run to catch the rain for showers. But in Galang II, there was a spring that had fresh, clear, cold water. When other kids showed it to me, I was so happy. It felt good and was not yellow like in Galang I. There were also wells where you could get fresh water, but mostly the adults did that because the wells were deep, and it was dangerous for a child to get too near. We loved well water.

In Galang II we had a little land to ourselves because of our house. In the backyard, there was room for my mom to grow vegetables. She did this with other ladies. Most women in my country know how to grow gardens. My mom planted hot pepper trees because my dad loves hot peppers. We would also give peppers to other people. She planted other vegetables too that we could eat, but I don't know their names in English. The food in Galang II was dispensed every two weeks instead of every month, and the kind of food varied each time. There were people who were not part of families, individuals whose allocations were not enough to sustain them. So my father would give them some of our family allotment because we usually had a little extra. There were several young men alone whose family had wanted them to escape, and those young men ate so much. Fortunately, there were many large families who could give them a little extra. At Galang II we had more vegetables. Every two weeks they would give us rice, eggs, green beans, and sometimes dried oysters. Sometimes the oysters had little white worms in them because they were so old. But we would wash them clean and cook them really well, and they tasted fine. It may sound disgusting, but the conditions over there were very different from here. You do what you have to do to survive. Some people broke out with red spots on their skin and got real itchy because of the food they ate, but I didn't. Often there wasn't enough to eat. So when they gave us something extra, we were glad to get it.

Upstairs in our Galang II house, there was no light. So we would put gasoline in a little drinking can, put a piece of cloth in the can, and make a little light. That's how we would study or read at night. We had to take safety precautions because lots of kids would get together at night and play games and cards by this dim light. For some games, if you lost, you had to kneel down. Sometimes instead of making the loser kneel down while playing, we would make the loser rub the soot from the bottom of the cooking pots on her face. It was all in good fun.

We celebrated the Vietnamese New Year over there too. We would pick banana leaves so that my mother could make the traditional dish, *banh tec.* It is made with sticky rice, green beans, and meat, covered with a banana leaf, and cooked for ten to twelve hours. We would wait overnight for the *banh tec* to cook. It was a very special event and fun watching the fire at night. Most people in the camp didn't do that.

Our teacher in Galang II was a Vietnamese. He taught us English, biology, and math, as in regular elementary school. In Vietnam I had been in the middle of the fourth grade, but in Galang II, I was in the fifth. If we did well in class, we could get a notebook with a Mickey Mouse picture on the front, something real colorful, or other school supplies such as a wooden pencil holder. I loved getting those prizes. When we left for America, we could sell them. They were worth something, and we could use them to buy some little snacks.

In Galang II, it was safer because the place where we lived was up on a hill. If something happened, it was usually because some hungry person had stolen food. There was not much violence. There was a TV outside where you could watch movies in Chinese but with English subtitles. I had some Chinese friends, so when we went to see a movie together, they would explain it to me.

There were also some markets in Galang II. There was a shoe market and a pants market. But we didn't have much money, and it cost a lot to buy those things. However, we did have some relatives who would send us a little money now and then. We would treasure that money so much. It would not mean much over here, but it meant a lot to us when we needed it most.

There was also a market in Galang I where you could buy fabric. Usually in our country, our people buy fabric and get a tailor to measure our waists and shoulders, and then we make clothes that fit us. We did the same thing in Galang. In Galang I my mother knew a market where both fabric and chickens were sold. So even after we left Galang I, we would sometimes go back to the market. If we wanted a shirt, we would go to market, buy the fabric, and get a tailor to make it our size. In our boat there were several people who were tailors. When we had to go somewhere special, such as to see the government officials, we would dress nicely. The girls would wear white shirts and light blue pants that fit us well. The earrings I wear now were made at Galang. At a jewelry store there, my mother had earrings made for each of my sisters and me.

There were several churches on the island, but we are not Christians. We're Buddhists. When I went in a Christian church, I was scared because I am not a Christian and I wasn't sure if it was right for me to go in. I have some cousins who are Christians, and they went to the church every Sunday. Outside the church there was a boat with a statue of Mary in it. I think it represented all the people who had survived in boats and come to that island. That church in Galang I was huge and white and lovely with the statue of Mary in front. I used to stare at it when I would pass by. I know it had power.

One time at this church they invited people to watch a movie about the life of Jesus and how he died, about the way people treated him when he was alive and how they killed him. I didn't know much English then, but I saw the pictures. I didn't really understand it, but later in America I happened to talk to a Christian lady who told me that her church used to sponsor a program on that island. I thought it was neat when I told her about my experience at the church.

In Galang I, there was also a band connected with the church. If you liked singing, you could go up on the stage with this band and sing, and kids would watch you. I used to watch one young lady from my boat practice singing. There was also a youth group there. I don't know if they were Christian, but there were kids who were orphans or whose parents didn't come with them. Some of them lived in the huge house by the church. They would go out into the woods and do things like Girl Scouts and Boy Scouts do here in America, but the boys and girls in the groups were mixed. They had a leader to guide them and lots of activities for them. People seemed to treat these orphans very well.

In addition to the Christian church, there was a huge Buddhist temple in Galang on top of a high hill with a big statue of Buddha in the center of it and a lot of smaller statues around the Buddha. If you wanted to visit this temple, you had to go a long way. There was also a Buddhist youth group, but I was not active in it.

One time in Galang I saw this man who had committed suicide. He had been in jail a long time. Even though I was afraid, I loved to look at new and strange things, so I ran to the jail when I heard that someone had killed himself. The man had something white coming out of his mouth, and a man who worked at the jail was saying that he had just seen the man looking okay only a few minutes before. Then they took him to the hospital morgue. Since I was curious about what that was like, I went there too. But soon I changed my mind and came back. You can see how free I felt to roam around the camp by myself. I felt safe.

I saw only a few Americans in Galang. Most of the people who took care of us were Indonesian. But when we began to do the paperwork to go to America, we met an American man. He had a Vietnamese secretary who translated for us. We would come to see him after they had reviewed our papers. After they evaluated your paperwork and they thought you could go up a level, you would come into the room to meet that American man. He seemed so tall to me then. I was scared because he was so tall. Though it was very hot in Galang, the air conditioner in his room made it very cold. I loved being in that air-conditioned room because it felt so good. It was like being in a refrigerator. I had heard there was air conditioning in America and had always wondered about it. But I didn't really believe it until I felt it in that man's office.

On a typical day, my mom cooked and did housework, and that kept her busy all day. She also went to school to learn English. At school she was glad to meet other ladies about her age because they all understood each other and could get support from each other. The teacher was a very nice Indonesian man. My father also attended a class. There were separate classes for men and women, but the children of both sexes went to school together. One time in my father's class the instructor asked, "Who in this room knows what 'hot dog' means?" Some people raised their hands and said they knew that "hot dog" referred to a dog that is hot. The teacher teased them and explained what it means in America. We didn't know there was such a thing as a "hot dog" in America.

When the time came to leave Galang II, we spent a few days in Singapore before leaving for the United States. At first, when I heard that we were going to America, I was very scared because it was the unknown and because I didn't know English. I told myself that in America, "Oh, of course, I will study in Vietnamese." This, I found out later, was far from true.

Chapter 7

The Norwegian Protector

Suzanne Tran Cheang graduated from Christian Brothers University in 1998 with a major in chemical engineering. She married and settled in the Dallas area, working for a pharmaceutical company.

In 1987, my aunt, Huong Tran, decided to leave Vietnam after her only child passed away. Her husband, Nanh Nguyen, had escaped by foot eight years earlier. Because she was alone, my aunt decided to take me with her. Even though I was only 12 years old, my family agreed to send me because they wanted me to receive the education that I needed and deserved. In Vietnam, I would not have been able to attend the school of my choice.

My aunt had already attempted an escape one month before she left with me. However, the Communist police found out about it and took some of the escapees into custody. Luckily, my aunt was not caught. A month later the owner of the same boat in which she had tried to escape before came to our house and asked if we were interested in another attempt. On the morning of August 2, 1987, my father took my aunt and me to Phuoc Khanh, where we pretended to be tourists. However, the police officers in that area watched every move that we made. After two days the police finally gave up on watching us. The third day, August 5, we left on a small fishing boat from Phuoc Khanh and were transferred later to a bigger boat. On the second boat we met 27 more people. The captain of this boat took us to Vung Tau, where we were to pick up another 50 people and more supplies. However, the police had captured that whole group and were waiting at Vung Tau to capture all of us. Somehow our captain found out about the police trap and was able to avoid it. As we moved out into the South China Sea, the Communist police spotted us and started chasing our boat. But we got into international waters before they could catch us.

We were on the ocean for four days and four nights. Since we hadn't been able to pick up our supplies in Vung Tau, we were running out of water and food by the third day. Also on the third day the engine broke down, but a diver on our boat saved us. He risked his life by getting under the boat without an oxygen mask to repair the engine. Within an hour, he had fixed it. Now our major concern was water. Everyone started to pray for rain, and that night our prayers were answered. I never thought I would be so happy to see rain fall. We stored the rainwater in whatever containers we could find.

During our four days on the sea, we saw a lot of ships, but none of them were willing to pick us up. After the fifth ship passed us, we had almost given up hope of being rescued. When we saw the sixth one, we waved at those on board but without any hope at all. Like every other ship before, it passed us by. Suddenly, the ship turned around and came back near us. Those on board signaled for us to move closer to them and then slowly lowered a rope ladder for us to climb aboard. Finally we were rescued, and everyone started to cry.

All the women and children were allowed to climb the ladder first. When I got on the ship, I thought I was floating in space because I could not feel the waves like I had in the small boat. I thought I was in heaven. But I woke to reality when I felt a hand searching me from top to bottom. Later on, the Norwegian captain apologized to all of us for having us searched. He told us that only a day earlier he had been robbed by pirates who he had thought were boat people. He hadn't stopped the ship to rescue us when he first saw us because he thought we were pirates too. But when he saw women and children, he realized that we were indeed boat people.

The captain arranged for all the women to stay on the top floor of the boat, where he stayed to protect us from any possible incidents. But the ship's crew treated us like their family. Some of them even gave us toys and clothes they had bought for their wives and children. The captain offered to take us back to Norway with him if we all agreed to go, but we were not able to go with him because all of us had family members elsewhere. We were sorry we couldn't go with him. Then he contacted the Japanese government and asked permission to drop us off there, even though Japan was farther away than any other refugee camp. We spent ten days and nights with the Norwegian captain and his crew. Everyone cried the day we left for the camp in Japan. As we left, the captain waved goodbye. I think I saw a tear rolling down his face.

Once we got on land, each of us was given an identical sweatsuit to wear so that the officials could recognize our group. Finally, on August 20, 1987, we reached the refugee camp in Tasaki, Japan. Here we were not allowed to go outside the camp without a staff member, but the camp itself was clean. Staff members were courteous to us and gave us food and a small allowance.

Four months later my aunt and I were moved to a different camp, in Nagoja Kimamoto. There we had more freedom. We were allowed to go anywhere we liked and were also allowed to cook our own food. Some of the men who stayed in the same camp with us were allowed to go outside to work. Every week a volunteer from the community came and taught us English. The camp staff also took us to places in Japan. We left this second camp after another four months. It was sad to leave the staff members because they were wonderful people.

Our third move was to Kumamoto, where we stayed our final four months before departing for America. I was happy to have things settled, but I was sad to leave behind so many good people who had helped me.

I came to the United States on June 7, 1988. My aunt was thrilled to see her husband again after nine years of separation. Because my family was still back in Vietnam, I was miserable for the first few years. But my aunt and uncle were there for me and loved me like their own child. They encouraged me and helped me get through the hard times. My aunt and uncle also helped me sponsor my family. After six long years, I was reunited with my mother and father, Do Cao and Liem Tran, my two sisters, and my brother. I truly believe that God has blessed me with two sets of wonderful parents, all four of them now with me in America.

Chapter 8

Drowning the Boat

Hung Truong settled in Blytheville, Arkansas, working as a
jewelry designer. He is married and has one son. Hung's special interests include fishing, painting, and playing guitar. He
graduated with an AA degree in art from MS County Community College in 1993. Hung is active in the Memphis Buddhist Association.

First, I want to tell you about the 1970s. Those were long years for my family. My family now has four boys and one girl, but in 1970, when I was five
years old, there was only me and my brother Dung. My mom was with us
then, and my daddy, Huu Truong, was in the South Vietnamese Navy. The
Viet Cong were fighting with South Vietnam in Da Nang, where we were
living. We could hear bombs and cannons every night. Then my daddy was
transferred to Saigon, but my mom, my brother, and I stayed in Da Nang
until my father found a place for us in Saigon. Soon the three of us rode a
helicopter to Saigon and moved into my father's house on Cuu Long Base.
In 1971, my mom had the third boy, Chien, and in 1973, the fourth, Thang.

My daddy built up the house on the base and tried to do everything
for my family, and my mom, Can Phan, was a real good mother—until
she left in 1973. At the time she was pregnant. Later I found out I had a
sister named Chau. Just after this, my father was sent to fight the Viet
Cong on an island somewhere. Because my mother had left and my father
was being sent somewhere else to fight, he sent us back to Da Nang, where
his sister lived. But my aunt had nine children of her own and could not
care for us. So in Da Nang we didn't have a house. All we had for a home
was a shelter we made from sticks and leaves. When we slept, we would

gather close to the sturdiest wall. We lived in these conditions from 1973 until 1974.

In 1973 I had problems with my uncle, my daddy's youngest brother. He had been in the military too and had been left handicapped when the Viet Cong shot him in one of his eyes. The military sent him home. I think my uncle was crazy because he tried to hurt my family. My aunt had to give him money to live at that time.

I was able to go only to the third grade in Da Nang and my brother to the second. In 1974, after my daddy finished his assignment, he told my aunt to send my second brother and me back to Saigon so that we could go to better schools. He sent my third and fourth brothers to live with my grandfather in Hue. So from 1974 to 1975, my second brother and I were in Saigon, but not usually together. I lived with different people around Saigon. Because of my daddy's military assignments, he was leaving all the time, and nobody was really taking care of me. I didn't live with my brother; he went to somebody else. He and I had to help the people we stayed with clean the house and take care of everything before we left in the morning to go to school. After school we did whatever they wanted. We worked for them so that we could live in their houses. In April 1975 when the Communists took over Vietnam, my daddy came home and took me and my second brother to a boat to try to escape Vietnam. After we rowed out to the boat, my father changed his mind. He said, "We can't go without your brothers." So we came back to the shore.

Soon the Viet Cong put my father in a reeducation camp to "clear his mind." After he got out of the camp, my daddy went back to Da Nang with me and my second brother. But my aunt still had her nine children and couldn't take care of my family. When we came back to Da Nang, we didn't have a house. We didn't have anything. My daddy had no money, only his two hands.

My two youngest brothers were still in Hue. My youngest brother could not walk. He did not have a mom, and he didn't have milk. Because there was no one to take care of him, he got sick. He couldn't see. He was like a starving African child. When my daddy and I came to Hue and saw my sick brother, my daddy cried and I cried too. We took my brother to Da Nang, where my father put him in the hospital. For about three months they took care of him at the hospital, and he recovered his eyesight. My family didn't have money, but my aunt had some to pay the hospital. When he got out, we didn't have money for a house. We had nothing. Even though my daddy was very sad about it, he had to send all four of us to an orphanage. We lived in the orphanage for about three months, and then my daddy made some money carrying loads for others on the street. With this money we rented a space in the front of a house owned by some other people. When we moved into that house, we had our first meal together in almost four years. Because I had been so often responsible for myself and the others, I knew how to cook and wash clothes for my little brothers and take care of everybody. So for a while we had a regular home again.

But in 1976, the Communists said all who did not have homes of their own had to go to what were called New Economic Zones. We were in the first group in Da Nang to go because my father thought that it would be a good new life for our family. But when we got there, we had to go to a very remote place, near Bien-Hoa, that was really terrible. When the trucks that took us let us out, I saw trees everywhere. I was frightened and I cried. My father was frightened too, but he didn't tell us that. In his mind he said: "God, what has happened to us? How will we live?" The people who drove us there told us to cut down the trees and build our own house. We only had two tools my daddy had brought with us from Da Nang and a couple of pans for cooking. It took us three months to cut some bamboo trees and make our house.

We lived there from 1976 through 1978 while my daddy worked in a group with a Communist leader. The workers cut down trees and cleared the land to plant rice. Then they would plant the rice, harvest it, and store it in big warehouses. The workers got some of this rice but not very much. If you didn't work, they would not give you rice at all. So every morning my daddy would get up at 5:00 A.M. to go to work and not come home until dark.

I went to school in this New Economic Zone. Because I was only 11 years old and in the fifth grade, my daddy wouldn't let me go to work. I said, "Daddy, let me go to work to help get some rice." But he loved me very much. He loved his children. He said: "No. No, child. Go to school." After school, I would cut trees with my second brother and try to help my daddy. We cleaned the yard, cut bamboo down, and planted tomatoes and corn, but we still did not have enough food. We would sometimes be so hungry that we would cut bamboo and boil the inside to eat. Sometimes we would get it out before it was done because we were so hungry. Sometimes we thought we would die. I have seen my daddy crawl on the floor and curl up like he was going to die.

This lack of food was because the group leader took everything for himself, mostly the rice. Everyone was afraid of him, and no one would speak up. But my daddy wrote a poem to tell everybody about what was happening there. My daddy spoke up. The leader got mad and came to beat my daddy up. My daddy fought back. When the leader asked my dad if he wanted to go jail, my daddy told him he talked a lot and he shouldn't be taking the rice. For a while the leader left him alone. But then the leader told the Communist police to come get my father. Four of them took him to the office and beat him all over his body. I didn't know what was going on. But when I went to school, I heard somebody say that my daddy was in the office. Usually if someone was taken to the office, that meant they would be beaten. I tried to run over there and help my daddy. They brought him outside and tied him to a tree. I went there and cried and cried. He said: "It's okay, child, okay. Go home and take care of your brothers." I went home and that afternoon my daddy told somebody to tell his child: "I'm going to jail. They are taking me to jail."

They put him in jail in the middle of nowhere, far from where we were. We didn't have rice. We didn't have anything to live on. We tried to cut bamboo shoots to eat. We went to other people to get manioc. We were begging. No one had any money. All we had was manioc for about a month.

At the time, the Communists would not let anybody get out of any New Economic Zone. Our zone had one main street, and it was closely guarded. If you tried to get out, they would shoot you. So we were trapped. But I heard of one lady who had hidden from the guards. She would get out very early in the morning, go around the main street, and crawl through the forest to a place where Vietnamese mountain people lived. She would get rice and fruit from these people and bring it back into the New Economic Zone and sell it for money. So I followed this woman through the forest and carried her rice and bananas for her. One day she gave me a bowl of rice, and I cooked it for my brother and me.

One time I cut down some trees and took some of the wood to school. Actually, I was doing two things: trying to get some money for wood while at the same time looking for my daddy. I told officials at the school that I needed to sell the wood so that I could buy some books and pants. The officials signed a paper to help me get past the guards on the main road. My friend and I carried the wood out to the guard and showed him the pass, but he didn't believe us. He said, "You're a liar." "But," I said, "it's true. Go to the school and check." So they took the paper. This was about 5:00 o'clock in the morning, and they checked it out until 11:00 o'clock. Then they told me: "It's okay. You can go."

So I walked down the road quite a while until I met a woman coming from the opposite direction, and she said, "Are you Huu's son?" When I said, "Yes," she said she knew where he was. I followed her directions and tried to find my daddy. People would say go over here and then go over there. When I finally saw him, we both cried. It had been two months since I had seen him. He said: "Okay, son. That's okay." He told the Vietnamese leader who was watching us and who saw us crying that I was his son. So the leader said he was going to let my daddy have three days' vacation to go home and see his sons.

As for my wood, I was lucky. I found someone to buy it early and made about 15 Vietnamese dollars. With this money I bought about eight pounds of rice. I was so lucky. I had found my daddy, and they were going to let him go home for three days. And I had some money. So I told my daddy to buy some meat. I told him, "I will cook and we will eat together."

At our house my daddy told us he didn't want his children living in the New Economic Zone. My brothers were thin, and their skin color was green because they didn't have enough protein in their bodies. I told him that we didn't have anything except our two hands and now some dollars I had earned. After three days my daddy told me: "We must get out of here and not come back. We must never let the children live in a Communist Zone anymore."

So the next night at about 1:00 A.M., the five of us went through the forest to Bien-Hoa. I carried my fourth brother on my back, and my second brother took my third brother's hand. My daddy carried the clothes and food. So we escaped from the New Economic Zone and the Communist jail. You see that our lives from 1975 to 1978 were not worth a penny.

After that, my daddy helped us all catch a train at Bien-Hoa to go to Da Nang. Because we didn't have enough money to pay for the trip to Da Nang, my daddy took a blanket and covered up my youngest brother. When the guy came to check for the tickets, my daddy said: "My son is hurt real bad. It's really terrible, and we don't have money. We are taking him for help." So he let us go.

After we got to Da Nang, we didn't have a place to live. My father was afraid that someone would go to the Communists and say that we were starving. He was afraid that the Communists would learn that he had escaped. If they knew that he had escaped from jail or that we all had left a New Economic Zone, they would kill my daddy. So my father said we must move near my grandfather, who lived 23 kilometers outside Hue.

There it was really terrible. We didn't have a house, so we started poor again. Because my daddy had to stay hidden to keep out of jail, he couldn't work to get rice. So he thought the only way out was for us to commit suicide. He wrote everybody a letter to say goodbye. He wrote one to my aunt in Da Nang. Three days later my father made a real good soup. It was going to be our last soup together because he put poison in the soup.

When my aunt got the letter, she traveled quickly to Hue. When she got there, she found my daddy cooking the soup. She kicked the soup pot over. She said, "Don't you ever do that." She said: "Why not let me take over your children? Why do you want to die?" My daddy said: "How can you tell me what to do? I don't know what to do. First, I get put in jail. Then I get out of jail. Maybe they will get me soon and put me back in jail. If I go to jail, what will my children do? How will they live?" My aunt made up her mind. She was going to get a boat, and we were all going to escape. She had some money, and in August 1979, she paid somebody to build a boat. She had nine children with her then, and she told my daddy: "Okay. I will let you go if you take four of my children with you. After you take my four children, I will bring your children with me."

At that time I didn't know that my daddy was planning to escape Vietnam. A letter came from Da Nang to Hue to my daddy, and I opened it. In it my aunt told my daddy how to go to Da Nang and escape Vietnam. I cried. I loved my daddy. My daddy told me: "Okay, son, the only way we can do better, the only way I can escape Vietnam and get to America, is this way. I would prefer you to come with me. I don't like it like this. I don't want you poor. I don't want you in a paper house." So I told my daddy, "Okay, I will take care of the kids." I was 14 years old.

My aunt's son came and told my daddy to get ready to go. At about midnight my daddy wrote me a letter telling me how to take care of my brothers, what I should do. I woke up at 5:00 the next morning, and he had already gone to Da Nang to take four of my aunt's children and escape Vietnam. My grandfather didn't want my father to go because if he went, my grandfather must take care of the children. My grandfather thought he was too old; he was about 70 or 75. My grandfather went to Da Nang to tell my daddy not to go, but when he got there it was too late. My father had already gone to Hong Kong with four of my aunt's children.

Soon he wrote a letter telling us that the Hong Kong officials had accepted them. He lived in Hong Kong for about five or six months, and then the Americans sponsored him to go to the United States.

Meanwhile we lived in Hue with my grandfather. Again we had started over, but still it was better than the New Economic Zone because there I didn't have relatives. Now my grandfather taught me how to farm rice. Also, I told my grandfather I would like to go to school, but he said, "You know your brothers don't have food to eat." So I didn't go to school. I would farm and dig the land every day to get rice and tomatoes and manioc. I tried very hard to learn from my grandfather. He was too old and couldn't work the farm. He just showed me how to do it. I worked on the farm, and every lunch, every dinner, I would cook only a small amount of rice with tomato. I didn't have money to buy pork, beef, or chicken. Every day we would have rice with tomato or rice with salt. I worked there for three years and cried every day. One day I saw airplanes in the sky, and I thought it was my daddy coming to pick me up. I dreamed about it. But it was not true. My daddy was in America, but he didn't have enough money to send to us yet. At that time, he was cleaning the Blytheville, Arkansas, courthouse for about three dollars an hour.

I continued to work on my grandfather's land until 1981, when my father's youngest brother came to see us. He is the one I told you about before, who had been blinded in one eye during the war. My uncle lived in Tay Ninh in the South close to the Cambodian border. He came up to Hue, got all four of us boys, and took us to live with him in Tay Ninh. We went by train to Saigon and then went southwest to his home.

My uncle lived in a New Economic Zone called Duong Minh Chau. It was much better than the New Economic Zone we had been in near Bien-Hoa. My uncle had a farm, but he didn't know how to work it. He wanted us to be his workers. I knew how to do everything, and I worked. But I let my brothers go to school. I didn't want them working because I knew my daddy wanted his boys to go to school.

My uncle had a wife and four children, but he didn't take care of them. I was taking care of my family and his family too. He didn't help me at all. Sometimes I was very tired of him and of the work.

Eventually my uncle wrote a letter to my daddy. He told my daddy that he was taking care of my family and that he wanted my daddy to send him money for taking care of us. My daddy sent about $500, and my uncle spent all of it. I was tired of the way he acted, but I didn't know what to do.

I worked on the farm in the daytime, but in the night I would go fishing in a nearby lake to make money for us. After I made $100 in Vietnamese money, I had enough for one pound of rice a day for me and my brothers. My eight- and nine-year-old brothers didn't know how to keep the rice secret, so one day my uncle and his wife found their rice and went crazy. They were yelling because the four of us had rice and had not given any to their family. But my uncle did not take care of his family.

This all happened one night when I was fishing. My uncle and his wife asked my brothers what they were cooking and eating, and the boys told them they were cooking rice with salt. Sometimes they would even have fish that I would bring home to eat with the rice. So my uncle asked them why I didn't tell him that we cooked fish with rice or cooked rice with salt. He asked why they lied to him, and he tied them up by their hands to a tree and beat them. There were many ants on the tree, and he let the ants bite them. At that time, I was fishing and didn't know about

Hung Truong (tallest) with his brothers Dung (next tallest), Chien (next), and Thang (youngest) in Vietnam, four months after their father left in 1979.

it until the morning. The whole village was talking about my family. I cried. I didn't know what to do. I was angry. I said: "Forget everybody. Forget my family, forget my uncle, forget my aunt—forget everything."

Meanwhile, my aunt had continued to live in Da Nang until after 1979, when my daddy escaped and the police came to her house. Because she was afraid the Communists would put her in jail, she moved to Saigon. After she moved to Saigon, she had a boat made and escaped from Vietnam in 1980 with her five remaining children. After some time in Hong Kong, she came with them to Blytheville, where my father lived with her other four children. When she arrived with her five children but not with any of his children, my daddy got so mad. He wanted to shoot the whole family. He said, "Why did you come with your children and not bring mine?" My aunt and her children were so afraid of him they moved to California.

While this was going on, I still lived there in Tay Ninh. I said to myself, "This is no life for my family." I felt the only way was to escape from Tay Ninh and go to Saigon, where my daddy had a friend. Of course, my uncle didn't want us to go because he was trying to make money from my daddy. My third and fourth brothers picked pecans and sold them so that we could have some money to get to Saigon. I wanted my second brother to stay in Tay Ninh long enough to get his high school diploma. But I took my third and fourth brothers with me to Saigon.

At first we rented a room in a villa in Saigon. Then I asked my daddy if he could send me money by way of the friend he had in Saigon. This was the first time that I got money from my daddy. It was $200 in American money. I took that money and bought a bicycle and rented a house. I let my brothers go to school. Usually everywhere I went in Vietnam I would go to work, and I would let my brothers go to school. I didn't want them to quit school. But in Saigon, I was able to go to school too. There was a night school for older students, and now I was in the seventh grade.

In the daytime some friends and I rode our bicycles to a town nearby called My Tho. There we bought rice and brought it back to Saigon to sell for a profit. But the Communists did not want anybody to go to My Tho and buy rice to take to Saigon. Two friends and I put our money together to buy rice in My Tho. We agreed that if one of us got caught, two guys would still have money and we would share that. One day the three of us went to My Tho. The police caught two of us but let one go. They took the other one's rice and his bicycle. They took him to police headquarters and kept him for four hours, treated him like a criminal, and then released him. Back in Saigon the police were looking for people who were selling rice. They came to my house to buy my rice with this cheap money. I had no choice but to sell it for this worthless money.

I kept thinking that this was not right. It was 1983, and still you could not make a penny. I said, "I've got to get out of here." So I sent a letter to my daddy and told him: "You must send me money. My brothers and I must get out of Vietnam." My daddy sent me $10,000 that he borrowed from a bank. Because he made only $3 an hour, some American people who adopted him said, "Okay, we will co-sign for you to borrow money to get your children out of Vietnam." But I did not use any of this money in the first attempt to get any of us out of Vietnam. This first attempt involved only Dung and Chien, my second and third brothers. By this time I was 18, and I had learned some things. I knew that many people were cheated out of their money when they tried to escape. So I told the people who were going to help my brothers escape: "If they get out and go to America, I will pay you money. If not, I will not pay."

Dung and Chien went to Phnom Penh, Cambodia, then to Kompong Som on the Cambodian coast, and eventually by boat to Klaeng, Thailand. It was nighttime when they got there, and some Thai soldiers shot at my brothers when they came ashore because the soldiers thought they were Cambodian Communists. They hit one of them in the arm. My brothers ran to the beach and hid. The next morning when the Thai were searching to see how many Communists they had killed the night before, they found my brothers. My brothers did not know how to speak Thai or English. The soldiers caught them and bandaged the injured one's arm and told them they had to go back to Cambodia. The Communists in Cambodia put them in jail in Phnom Penh, but they escaped and returned to Saigon.

After we were all reunited in Saigon, I bought a small boat and began to make it bigger. It was originally about 12 meters long and 2 meters wide. I put together a new engine, and I fitted everything into the boat.

Meanwhile I worked for the Communists for three years, from 1983 to 1986. There was a river between Saigon and the coastal town of Vung Tau, and the Communists wanted someone to guard the trees along the river, to keep people from cutting them down. So I patrolled the area for the Vung Tau Communists. This job paid very little.

During this time, even though my father had sent me a large amount of money, I still dressed like I was poor and acted like I was poor. But one day my uncle from Tay Ninh came to Saigon. He wanted me to help him with money and tried looking for me, but I hid from him. I didn't want to see him. He told my relatives that he wanted to see me only one more time.

I'll tell you why he wanted to see me one more time. It was because he said he was poor, and his children had been sick and in the hospital, and he didn't have any money. So I helped him with some money to live. He also said he wanted to see my brothers. After he came to my house and saw my brothers he told me: "I know you are making a boat to get out of Vietnam. If you don't give me money to live, I will tell the police you are making a boat to escape." I said: "That is ridiculous. Why do you make trouble for me?" Then I gave him about $50, but he said that wasn't enough. Then I gave him $100. After $100, he said okay and left. My uncle went out the door and straight to the police.

One night a friend who knew about this told me I had to hide because the police would be looking for me. So I went to my friend's house to sleep. Three policemen with AK-47s came to my house looking for me. My brothers were there, but the police didn't bother them.

The Saigon policemen didn't know about my job in Vung Tau because the Vung Tau police didn't communicate with the Saigon police. I worked for the Communists in Vung Tau, but they didn't know about my history because my boat was registered in my friend's name, not mine. I didn't want to let them know who I was.

Usually the Communists didn't work in Vung Tau on the weekends. Instead they would go back to Saigon. This made the weekends in Vung Tau the best time to plan an escape. A friend in Saigon brought my three brothers and now also my sister to Vung Tau on a Saturday afternoon. On May 30 in the dark of the night, I got everybody on the boat and waited for the tide to come in because the water was too low for us to leave then. I waited until 1:00, 2:00, 3:00, 4:00, 5:00—still the water was not high enough. I said, "God, this is killing me." Soon it was light, and I said to those hoping to escape with me: "Okay, you must return to Saigon because today we cannot escape. The sun is already up." So everybody went home.

After another week we gathered again in Vung Tau to try to escape. We jumped on the boat again, and at 2:00 in the morning, I pulled the boat out. I had ten people on board: five from my family (my three brothers, my sister, and myself), three from my friend's family, and two others, a husband and wife from Vung Tau who knew which way we should go. The boat had a one-cylinder engine and a deck I had added. It was about four feet from the deck to the bottom of the boat.

By 4:00 in the afternoon we were in the South China Sea and had gone far around Con Son Island to avoid the many boats that stayed near there. But the men on one boat saw us, and they knew we had escaped from Vietnam, so they followed us. They took three AK-47s and shot in our direction. We were crying, we were so scared. They told us we must stop. We said to each other: "We can't stop. We must run." But my boat was too small to run very fast. And they had a big boat, about 50 feet long. They shot around us. Everyone but me was under the deck. I was saying: "God, I don't know why they don't let me go. If they catch me, they will take me back and shoot me." They were shooting all around us, too near. It was like rain. Finally, I said: "Okay, stop. Let them do what they want to do. If we don't stop, they will kill everybody." So I stopped, and they came to the boat. They asked: "Why didn't you stop? Don't you know we shot three boxes of bullets already. Wonder who will pay for the bullets?" I told them: "I am really sorry. I'm very sorry. I just want to escape from Vietnam. I don't want to come back. I am afraid of you. If you catch me, I don't know what to do."

They said: "You must stop. Why didn't you stop? How many people are on the boat?" I said: "Only ten people, and we are in families. We don't have anybody else." They said: "You are lying. Your boat must have about 20 or 30 people under that deck. You must have a lot of money." Mainly they wanted money from us. I said: "I only have ten people on the boat. If you want to see, go down and look around." So they went down and looked and then told me to get on their boat. They told me: "What are you going to do? Do you want to come back to Vietnam?" I said: "Everybody wants to get out of Vietnam. They never want to come back. I'm sorry about that. If you let us go, God will bless you. If you don't let us go, we don't know what to say." So they said, "Okay, there is just one little thing." They meant gold. They wanted several grams of gold. But I told them: "I don't have gold. I have only these rings on my hands, and I have a small electric watch." I told everybody to take their jewelry off and give it to them because we didn't need the money. We needed to go. So everybody gave me their money and their gold, and I gave it to them, and they said: "It's not enough. We're going to take you back." So they attached a rope to our boat and pulled us back toward Vung Tau. When we got about halfway back to Vung Tau, they said that if we had money, and we were ready to give it to them, they would let us go. Again we told them, "We don't have money." And this time they let us go. Although they took several rings and a chain from me, they let me keep one ring and my watch. After that I was very happy. I said, "Thank you very much." Everybody said, "Thank you." They said "good luck" and left.

Then we spent our first night on the sea. Water was everywhere. Maybe 24 hours later, after we had decided to go west, I saw a real bright light on a boat. Then I saw that it had many lights. I said, "We have to turn on our lights." But our boat was too small, way too small, like a small dot on the sea. They couldn't see the boat or our lights and went away.

On the second day, the boat was running okay. I checked the oil and the water. Then I cooked rice, and everybody ate.

Also on the second day, we came near Kuala Terengganu in western Malaysia, but we had a problem. There were too many Thai boats around. The first one we met was at 10:00 A.M. on the second day. I saw one boat turn around and come by us. They looked like Thai pirates. They jumped on my boat, and they asked, "Do you need water or fish or rice?" I said: "Yes, give me some. Help me go to Thailand." They said: "No, the Thai don't want you now. Go to Malaysia." They told me to give them a ring or a watch. So I gave them my last ring and my watch. They gave us fish and rice.

Still on the second day there were 15 or 20 boats around us. We didn't know which were fishermen and which were pirates. At about 4:00 a silver boat with the number three-three-seven-three (3373) came by my boat. I thought it was like the first boat, or that maybe they were going to give us some water and help us go to Thailand and the refugee camp. That's all we needed. Instead this guy jumped down to my boat and hit me on the head right away. I fell down, and about six people jumped on my boat. They took our long knives, attacked us, and tried to wreck my boat. They told us to take off all of our clothes. Then they searched us and got our money. They took almost everything off the boat. They took the lights, the cigarettes, the food. They tore my engine apart so much that they thought it would not run anymore. After they took everything, they beat everybody real hard. I thought I was going to die. I don't know how I was still conscious. We were all crying. I said, "Oh, please, let us go." After the pirates took everything and left, they used their big boat to hit my boat. I got my engine started and ran away from that boat. After we had run away from that boat for about five minutes, our boat stopped. I didn't know what was going on with the engine. So I went down to check it out. The Thai had taken out part of the oil pipe, and I couldn't start it again.

At that time, we were tired. We were worn out, and everybody lay on the boat and slept from 7:00 P.M. until 4:30 A.M. At 4:30 it was still dark outside, but now there were bigger waves on the ocean. I thought that a thunderstorm was coming. I couldn't start the engine. Because the battery no longer worked, we had to try to start it by hand. I looked at the sky and how dark it was and how huge the waves were getting. I was praying. We were going up and down. I was real scared. I prayed to God, then I went down and tried to start the engine again. I said: "I must start the engine. If the engine doesn't start, the waves will turn the boat over and kill everybody." I tried to start it again and again. I was tired and wanted to quit, but my friend said: "Hung, you must try. If you don't try, the storm will kill everybody." So I started again. I prayed, "God, help me." And the engine started. After it started, my friend went to the front and tried to jump up and down to keep the boat straight.

The thunderstorm was from 7:00 A.M. until 3:00 P.M. By 1:00 I stretched my body across the deck and tried to balance the boat. It didn't matter where the boat went as long as I could keep the water from coming into the boat. I went to the front and stuffed clothes in places, trying to keep the water from getting into the boat. Then I'd go back to balancing again. Sometimes I used my hands to cover my face. The rain was driving real hard. It was like somebody took sticks and beat my face real hard. I prayed to God and said, "If you will help me come to the land, I swear to God that I will be real good, and I will cut off my hair."

After about 15 minutes, I saw a small light. I didn't know what it was. I didn't know if it was an island or what. As our boat came nearer to the light, I saw that it was an oil rig out in the ocean. I shouted at the men on board a big boat near the rig and asked them where they were from. They said that they were from Indonesia and that we must go back north about two days and one night to get to Pulau Bidong.

But we were worn out. They gave us some water and some biscuits and told us to go. I said: "All the people are tired and hungry and sick. They need a doctor. If we go out there for two more days, and have another thunderstorm, it will kill us." I said to the women, "Go and jump on the big boat." Then the men jumped on the boat. Finally the people on the boat came out and helped us. They got the doctor to tend to the women. They gave us rice and chicken soup. Then they told us: "All right, we have helped you for about five hours. You can also stay here overnight, but tomorrow morning you must go back to your boat and leave." I said, "Oh, my God, we can't leave." I talked to my friend and said: "We can't leave. What can we do?" And he said, "I don't know what to do." So we slept in the nighttime. But then my friend said: "I know what to do. At 6:00 in the morning, we can go to the boat and open a hole to let water come into the boat."

Early in the morning, they told us to go. I went down and said: "Oh God. Water is coming into this boat. We can't go." They said, "Oh, there's too much water!" So they took their pump in and sucked the water out. After they sucked the water out, I told them that because the Thai pirates had hit the boat, it had a hole in the bottom. That was why we couldn't go. At least it was true that there was a hole in the bottom. All the workers wanted was to keep us from going to Indonesia.

Because their boat was so large, they took a great big rope and pulled

Getting supply of water at refugee camp, Pulau Bidong, Malaysia, 1987.

my boat up out of the water and onto the big boat to repair it. They took the engine apart, cleaned it, and put it back together. They fixed the old boat for us. We stayed there three days. That was the sixth day after we had escaped.

Then they told us that they would take us to another oil rig in Malaysia that was owned by the same company. Their boat traveled about 50 miles an hour. It took them from 7:00 A.M. to 7 P.M. to get within a mile of the other oil rig, a very long trip. If it took them that long, I don't know how they thought I could get to Pulau Bidong in two days, because my boat couldn't go fast like that.

When we came within a mile of the rig, they put my boat down and told us to get in the boat and go to the Malaysian oil rig. We said, "Thank you." For three days they had helped us, and they had brought us to the oil rig. When we arrived in our little boat at the second oil rig, we said, "Please help us." Those on top of the oil rig said, "No, no." They didn't want to accept us either. So I tied my boat to a big boat near the oil rig. And I waited until midnight. I told everybody to go up onto the oil rig. They were crying. But they climbed up any way they could. They went up to the first floor and then to the second.

When I saw that they were safe, I took my big hammer and I hammered out the floor. As I hammered, I cried. I told that boat: "That's my friend. That's my heart." Because that boat had helped me escape from Vietnam. It had helped me get away from pirates and get away from the thunderstorm. After that, I jumped on the rig, and I watched the boat go down into the water. I cried, and then I said: "That's okay. Thank you." And then I jumped onto the first floor of the oil rig and climbed to the second.

At about 2:30 in the morning, a thunderstorm started coming. I didn't know what would happen if we stayed where we were, so we climbed to the third floor. When the workers on the top saw us below, they threw a big sheet of nylon down to us. We covered ourselves with the nylon until 6:00 A.M., when the storm went away.

By 7:00 that morning it was quiet. The people came down and helped us. They gave us some food. One guy told us we could stay there three days. Then a big boat could come and take all of us at one time to Pulau Bidong. While I was on this rig, I wrote a letter to my daddy. My daddy later said that when he got the letter, he cried and cried and told everybody that his child had come to Pulau Bidong in Indonesia. (He thought Pulau Bidong was in Indonesia.) The trip to Pulau Bidong took one day and one night.

We thought that life in the camp would be good. At that time, in 1986, there were about 3,000 Vietnamese at Pulau Bidong. In the camp they gave us medicine and a house. I had a small house, about four meters around, but it didn't have walls. It had a roof. There were rats that would come out at night and bite us. There were small animals and insects from the woods that would bite everybody. I lived there about one month. Then someone from the United Nations wanted us to go to Thailand and identify the boat of the pirates who had attacked us. So after one month, we went to Thailand to give information, but we couldn't identify the boat or the people because they couldn't find them. So we returned to Pulau Bidong and lived there for about three months. During our time at Pulau Bidong, I shaved my head to keep the promise I had made to Buddha during the terrible storm. Shaving my head marked the beginning of a special period of devotion to Buddhism.

After three months, my daddy did the paperwork to sponsor all of us to go to the United States. Before, he had done the paperwork for four sons, but not for my sister, Chau, because he didn't know she was coming with us. After I came to Pulau Bidong and he put Chau on the paperwork, the American government did not believe him. So they told him he must have a blood test and everything must be checked out before we could go.

After three months of living at Pulau Bidong, they sent us to Sungei

Hung Truong's sister, Chau, at the Memphis airport in October 1989, being met by her father, Huu Truong.

Besi, a better refugee camp. In Sungei Besi we went to school and to our Buddhist temple. I was a boys' leader in the temple. I tried to help everybody, especially on New Year's and on Buddhist Memory Day.

In refugee camps like Pulau Bidong and Sungei Besi, you couldn't eat pork because Malaysia is a Muslim country. If you ate pork, they would shave your head and put you in jail for one month. They didn't let us cook in our houses either. They just cooked outside for about ten people, and they cooked terrible food. But Sungei Besi was better than Pulau Bidong because the house was better. When my daddy could, he would send us money, and we would buy food at the little Malaysian store. Then we would hide at home and cook.

After three years in the camps, we found out we could go to the United States. My father still lived in Blytheville, Arkansas, and he counted every day. On October 24, 1989, after ten years and two months, we saw our father again in the Memphis airport. We were on "Channel 13 News" and in the newspaper too.

You may wonder how my sister came to escape with us. If you remember, after my daddy left in 1979, I was working the farm with my grandfather. On New Year's 1980, my grandfather gave me the money to buy new clothes. I remember this so well because that was the first time since 1973 that my brothers and I had been given brand-new clothes. Since 1973 we had worn those clothes every New Year. Every year my father would make them larger. I would give my clothes to my second brother. His clothes would go to my third brother, and his clothes would go to the fourth brother. Every year it changed like that. If it didn't fit, we made it larger. Everything my daddy or my mom bought for me I still kept a long time. So in 1979, for the first time since 1973, my grandfather gave me the money to buy new clothes for New Year's. At that time I was 14, and my daddy had just escaped from Vietnam.

I talked in my mind: "I need new clothes? What for? My life is nothing. I don't have a mom. I don't have a father. I need clothes? What for?" So I hid from my grandfather and took that money and used it to catch a train to Saigon so that I could find my mom. I wanted to tell her to come back and live with my family. In Saigon I found some relatives who showed me where my mom lived, and I went to her house and saw her.

By that time, she had already gotten married. She had one child and was pregnant with her second child. I don't know how she was feeling, but I saw her, and I was feeling like I had really lost my mom. I lost my daddy and I lost my mom. I didn't have anybody to take care of me. The only thing to do was to go back to Hue and take care of my brothers. I told my mom: "It's over. Okay. From 1973 to 1980 is seven years. I have

Hung Truong's family in Blytheville, Arkansas, Christmas 1990.

seen you. You are married, and you can't take care of my brothers. You must take care of your new family."

I left her and caught the train and thought about my mom and dad over and over again from Saigon to Hue, about two days and two nights. I thought a lot. I got to Hue, and I went around Hue City. I didn't go back to my grandfather's house yet. I spent time in the afternoon wandering around the city. It was so beautiful. It reminded me of my daddy because I used to go around with him in the city every afternoon when we came into town. I went to some of the places where my daddy would go. I tried looking everywhere to see my daddy, but I didn't see him. That night I slept by the front door of somebody's house and dreamed I saw my daddy. In my dream he told me: "Hung, it's okay. It's okay. You're going to have to take care of your brothers. I will help. I will sponsor you. Don't worry." I woke up but didn't see my daddy. The next day I walked around the town again and then jumped on the bus and came back to my grandfather's farm.

Three years later, in 1983, when I moved from Tay Ninh to Saigon, I went to see my mom again and said to her: "My daddy told me I have a sister. Where is she?" My mom said that she bore my sister in 1974 and then let somebody keep her because at that time she couldn't take care of the child. I went looking for my sister and found her where my mom had told me to look. I told the lady who kept her, "That's my sister." And she accepted it. I told my sister that someday I would make a boat, and I wanted her to escape with us.

So when I escaped Vietnam in 1989 at age 24, I took Chau with me. Now she is married and lives in Hot Springs, Arkansas, with her husband and little girl. Dung, my second brother, and my father live in California, and Chien and Thang live in Memphis. I live with my wife and child in my father's house in Blytheville.

Chapter 9

Out of San Diego and into Saigon

Be Van Vo and his wife, Phon Neang, settled in Memphis with their four children and his mother. Be is a die-cut operator at Americraft. Phon works at a lumber company in Horn Lake, Mississippi. In his spare time, Be likes to do woodworking.

In April 1975 as Saigon was falling to the Communists, I was at the Naval Training Center in San Diego, California. I was a lieutenant junior grade in the South Vietnamese Navy. My trainers asked me if I wanted to stay in San Diego or go home to Vietnam. When I told them I wanted to go home, they said: "Why don't you want to stay here? If you go back home, you will be in danger. You will be killed. You need to stay here." But I told them, "My family, my relatives, my country is over there, not over here."

Back in 1970 I had gone through Officer's Candidate School in Newport, Rhode Island. After completing OCS, I went back to Vietnam, where I was commissioned an officer in the South Vietnamese Navy. In January 1975, the South Vietnamese Navy sent me back to the United States for training, this time to San Diego. On April 23, 1975, I left San Diego to return to Vietnam. I arrived in Saigon on April 24, and one week later all of Vietnam became Communist.

The first thing they did was call up all those who had been officers in the South Vietnamese military to go to reeducation camps to study for 30 days. At least that's what they said. I was to present my name and my personal history to them. After I did this, I wound up in different reeducation camps for a total of five years. Every six months or year, I'd be

86

moved to another camp. The first camp I went to had about 10,000 people in it. For the first six months I did nothing. Then they made us work eight hours a day, six days a week, with only one bowl of rice and salt three times a day. Sometimes I ate crickets to keep from starving.

Since I had been in America a couple of times, they said I belonged to America. In fact, when I first came back to Vietnam, they said I was part of the CIA. I told them: "No. I came back to be with my family. I knew that the war was over." But they didn't believe me.

In 1981 when I was released from the camps, the Communists still didn't believe me. They wouldn't let me get a job, and they didn't want me to live inside Saigon. They wanted me to leave Saigon and go instead to Can Tho, where I had been born on October 28, 1949. But I knew I could never make enough money there to live. So I stayed in Saigon, but even there we were very poor. Almost everything in our house had been sold.

Every morning in Saigon my wife sold sticky rice, and I would do any job I could find, like painting or woodworking. I would work for whoever could pay me. I did this until Christmas 1981, when I first tried to escape. Because I had been a naval officer, I knew how to navigate a boat. Some people who wanted to leave Vietnam asked me to lead their group from Rach Gia, but the Communists caught me there and everyone else on the boat, about 100 of us. The motor on the boat had not even been started yet.

Even though the Communist police put me in jail, it was easier there than at the reeducation camps because there was more food to eat. They kept me in jail for nine months and finally released me in September 1982.

When I went back to my house in Saigon, the police kept their eyes on me because they knew what I could do. The second time I was more careful. I went out from Saigon to Vinh Long about ten times. I would go out but would come back if I saw local police. The plan was to move from a small boat to a big boat that had enough provisions. We waited on a small boat to pick us up, but it didn't come. We waited and waited. At around midnight we went back home. We hid and waited the next night too, but I didn't believe the boat would come. In the morning the police found us hiding in the bushes. The police asked me: "Why are you trying to leave Vietnam? Do you want to be an American?" I said: "No, I just want to be free. If I could get a job, I would stay. What I'm doing, I'm doing for my family. I have to make some money."

As punishment for this second escape attempt, they put me in jail for a month and a half. They beat me hard this time and took off all my clothes and took everything I had on me. After they released me, I went back to Saigon. By this time, I didn't want to try anymore. My wife said

Be Van Vo (far left) in English class, Bataan, 1987.

to me, "No, stop here." But my aunt and her husband wanted me to try again. I said, "Let me think." After a couple of months, I said, "Okay."

This time I went to Can Tho, my birthplace. My wife and children were still in Saigon with my mother. My plan was to sponsor them once I got to America. I knew that was a safe way to move my family from Vietnam. If I brought them with me on the boat, it would not be safe. If I died on the sea, my family would still be alive. Sometimes whole families died on the sea. I didn't want that.

So I went to Can Tho where my aunt's relatives already had a boat with provisions. Unlike most people, we started out with a large boat. It was an open boat about 4 meters wide and 20 meters long and made of metal, not wood. It had one motor, no water pump, and one spare battery to start the motor.

My aunt's relatives and I left Long Phu on April 27, 1986, at 8:00 A.M. They had told me there would be no more than 45 people going. More than that is dangerous. But when I met the others, I found out that the total on our boat was 114. Because of the size of the boat, though, you could not see the people when they were hidden. Because there was no deck,

Be Van Vo in Manila, 1987.

we put plastic on the top, and on top of that, we put sand and bricks, with the people under all this. It was so hot they couldn't wear clothes, and of course, there was no place to go to the bathroom.

After we got out on the sea, we put a plank on the top, and you could walk on that. That gave us more room. Also, we had plenty of food and water.

At about 4:00 A.M. on April 30, we met an oil rig. They gave us some more food and showed me the direction to Pulau Bidong off the coast of Malaysia. As we neared the area the oil rig workers had described, I saw lots of small islands, but I wanted to land on a big island. At about 8:00 P.M. I saw a light on an island and went toward it. An hour later we were on Pulau Bidong.

I was in the Pulau Bidong camp for three months. It was rough, but they did have meat. However, you couldn't legally eat pork. The Chinese might sell you the head of a pig for one American dollar. If you bought it, cooked it, or ate it and got caught, the camp officials would shave your head and put you in jail. That wasn't a problem for me because I had no relatives in another country to send me money for pork or anything else.

After those three months on Pulau Bidong, I spent three weeks in

Phon Neang and Be Van Vo with their family on arrival in Memphis, 1993.

the Sungei Besi transit camp before leaving for the Philippines. I was there seven months and served as an assistant teacher during that time.

I arrived in Memphis on March 30, 1987, almost one year after I had left Vietnam. As soon as possible, I filled out the necessary documents with Catholic Charities to sponsor my family. In 1993 my wife and four children arrived, and in 1994 my mother arrived. During the time between my arrival and my family's, I sent them money that I made here. That way they had enough food and clothes.

Someday I'd like to visit Vietnam with just my wife, not my children. Before I go, I want to be sure all my children have graduated from high school and can take care of themselves. A lot of people I know have gone back to Vietnam to visit and seemed to do okay. They were able to come back to the United States. But I have less reason to go than most. My father is dead, and my mom is here with me. If I went back, it would be to see my friends.

Chapter 10

Vung Tau, Pulau Bidong, and Bataan

Binh Le (pseud.) studied marketing at Christian Brothers University in Memphis, where at the time of this writing he was living with his parents, two brothers, and a sister. Binh has asked that a fictitious name be used to protect his identity.

Because my father had been a soldier of the former Vietnamese government, we weren't treated very well. In 1975, my father was put in a reeducation camp for six years, but even when he got out, the police kept watching him. That was one reason my parents wanted to escape. Another reason they wanted to leave was so that my nine brothers and sisters and I would have a chance to go to school. In Vietnam we had no chance of getting a good education, certainly no chance for higher education. Although we had shelter and enough food to get by, my parents wanted a better future for us. They felt that in Vietnam we had no future.

To escape by boat was the only way to get what we wanted, but we didn't get out on either our first or second try. During the first attempt, we were on the shore but hadn't gotten to the boat yet when the police came. That time we were able to elude them.

In 1982, all of our family got on a boat and were at sea for five days. But that time we did get caught. The police used their boats to pull us back to Camau, where they put us in prison for three months. The whole family, even the two-month-old baby, was put in prison. We slept on the dirt floor with everything from ants to rats crawling around us. The Communists gave us vegetables to eat, but they didn't wash the food. They chopped up the vegetables, put them in a pot, and cooked them for us. But I guess we got used to it because we didn't get sick.

Later that same year, my two older brothers tried to escape but disappeared at sea. We never saw them again. Even now my mom cries every time we mention them. It creates a gloom in us and makes us hate the Communists even more. Also, a few months after my older brothers disappeared, my parents lost their newborn son.

After our second unsuccessful attempt, the government took our home away—took everything we had. When we got out of prison, we slept on the street for two or three months. We didn't have money. We didn't have anything. My father finally cut down little trees and put up a small lean-to for us to sleep in. It took us two years to go from living in a lean-to to living in a regular house again. In Vietnam, it's not like here, where everybody has to have a house. There you can just cut something in the jungle, drag it up to a space, and build something.

Although getting caught and imprisoned frightened us, we weren't too frightened to try again. Like a lot of other people, we would rather have died than stay in Vietnam. The conditions were that bad.

We finally made our successful escape in 1984. We had no other way than escape by boat. Unless you had immediate relatives in the United States or in another country who could file a petition to sponsor you, there was no other way out. Escape was our only alternative.

My father's family was originally from the North. However, in 1945 the Communists took over the North, and my grandfather went to the South to get away from them. Then, in 1975, the Communists came into the South and gained control of all of Vietnam. So for their whole lives, my grandparents on my father's side have run away from the Communists.

It took over a year to prepare for our third escape attempt. Our first task was to buy a wooden fishing boat with a deck and small cabin. Then we would go out in the boat so that we could learn how to get around in it. But we did actually fish. We had to do whatever other people did, going in and out from the shore every day so they wouldn't suspect us. We had to practice over a year, getting to know the area. Fortunately, my hometown of Vung Tau is on the coast, about two hours southeast of Saigon.

All we did that year was learn to live as fishermen. We gathered supplies for the escape a little bit at a time and stored them because we could not transport many things to hiding places at one time or the police would know we were escaping. We gathered dry food, water, and of course gasoline. We buried some of the supplies under the bushes on the coast so that we could dig them up when it was time to leave. We couldn't put much on our boat until it was time to leave because the police would become suspicious.

To increase our chances of leaving without being detected, we had to escape during the night. During the day before the escape, we dressed as if we were going out to work. Then we went to some huts and stayed there until about 2:00 or 3:00 in the morning. To get from the huts to the boat was not easy. As we went through the jungle in the dark, our clothes were torn and our bodies cut by briers. I even lost my shoes.

One hundred and eight people escaped on that boat, including my father, my two sisters, one of my brothers, and myself. My mother stayed home with three remaining brothers.

Once on board we tried to set out, but soon something went wrong with the boat motor. Back on the shore, some men helped us with the motor, but even after being fixed, the motor was very slow. Finally, on June 16, 1984, we got away from the coast and headed into the South China Sea, moving toward Malaysia.

We were on the sea for six terrible days. The first few days I didn't know much because I was seasick. We were all seasick. Only my dad and a few men were well enough to be awake and know what was happening. Most of the children and women were lying about as if they were dead.

At first two men on the boat used a compass and maps to navigate. But on the third day out, one of them was washed overboard in a big storm. The water was washing over and over the boat. We had two machines to pump it out, and we were all bailing too. Suddenly the navigator washed overboard. My father turned the boat around to look for him, but all we saw was a flashlight. There were many storms like this while we were at sea.

My father had been steering the boat for six days with hardly any break when he first sighted an island. In his excitement, he called everybody up from below. When we saw the island, we were all so happy and jumping up and down. We agreed that regardless of what country the island belonged to, we would try to land there. We had all heard stories about coming to islands that would not accept you. But we were out of gas and food and counting our water drip by drip. My father beached the boat so that we couldn't be turned away. If we had spent more time on the sea, we would have died.

When we first landed, we didn't see any people. Then soldiers came out and put a rope enclosure around everyone and forced us to take off all our clothes for inspection, all of us—men, women, and children. After they checked us, they took us to a long building with about 15 rooms. Fortunately, our five family members were able to stay together.

We had landed on Pulau Bidong in Malaysia, and the conditions there were bad. There were public bathrooms, but they were very dirty. Rats as big as cats would bite your fingers at night while you slept. Most of the food was imported from the mainland and was often rotten. Every week they gave each of us seven packs of noodles. When they gave us chicken, it smelled, but we had to eat it because there was nothing else. Once I was so sick I almost died. My dad took me to a little clinic near the headquarters for help.

One thing we did get at Pulau Bidong was education. At age nine, I began classes. It was the first time I'd ever gone to school, and I loved it. Even though I had a hard time at first, I soon loved to make the honor roll. Many of my friends had the same chance to go to school, but they didn't value it so much. Going to school was the best thing in the camp for me. I had been through so much that caused me to value my education. Now I really appreciated the educational opportunity I had in Pulau Bidong. I just wanted to learn.

One of our most important subjects was English, but we had no native speakers as teachers. Instead they were Vietnamese, and they taught us mostly British English. Still English was my favorite subject. In camp it was fun to learn English because no one knew it. The class would laugh about it and have so much fun learning different words that sounded so weird.

There were also churches in the camp: Catholic, Baptist, and Buddhist. Because I was a Catholic back in Vietnam, I got into the youth group at the Catholic church. During the three years I spent on Pulau Bidong, different priests would come to serve the church and would stay a month or so and then leave. Whether we had a priest or not, I spent most of my time at church working on different projects. It was at Pulau Bidong that I had my confirmation and first communion. But because we had to wait for a bishop, we weren't actually confirmed for two more years. For a year or so, the Malaysians would not let any priests come over from the mainland because they did not like Catholics. Also, when we had communion, we had only bread because they wouldn't allow us to have wine.

Even though the conditions on the island were hard, living there was still a lot of fun. I remember my years there as the best years of my life. Even though there wasn't enough food to eat or enough clothes to wear, we felt free. It was a whole different world from Vietnam.

But I was a child and perhaps saw some things as better than they were. The Malaysian army was based there, and they beat some of the boat people. The Malaysians in general were not friendly, but the U.N. workers were very good to us.

In the camp there were two 20-inch color televisions for about 10,000 people. Because television was totally new to me, I loved it. Since the programming was in Chinese, Malaysian, and Indian, we just had to do the best we could to understand. My dad liked the Indian movies because they were more conservative than the other programming.

Getting approval to leave Pulau Bidong was difficult for my family. Because we had no relatives anywhere to sponsor us, we had to stay in the camp for three years. At the end of those three years, a U.S. representative called us for an interview. Even though we told him we had no relatives, he still took us because United States Catholic Charities agreed to sponsor us. Two weeks passed between the time the United States representative told us that we were accepted and the time we actually left. When we were told we would be leaving Pulau Bidong and would eventually go to live in the United States, we couldn't believe it. But we knew we would have to go first to the Philippines for six months of language and cultural preparation. As the time to leave Pulau Bidong drew near, I was frightened and didn't want to leave my friends. We were so close. By letter and sometimes by phone, I'm still in contact with two who live now in France and others who live in the United States.

We got to the Philippines first by boat and then by plane. We went on a boat to the Malaysian mainland, then took an air-conditioned bus with a TV to the airport at Kuala Lumpur. The bus ride took so long that I got motion sickness, but there were bags on the bus. The Kuala Lumpur airport was very large. It was so clean and nice I thought it was paradise. I had heard of planes and had seen pictures, so I wasn't frightened. In fact, I was really excited.

The plane took us to Bataan, Philippines, where we went through the inspection process, this time with our clothes on, and were put into a long building again. But this one had partitions and was clean. Our building even had its own restroom. We were to stay here for six months.

You may wonder whether we were ever in contact with my mother and the brothers still back in Vietnam during the time we were in Malaysia and the Philippines. At Pulau Bidong we got to write letters to Mom, but we didn't have any stamps to mail them, so we would save packages of noodles for a week to buy a stamp. I cried every time I read Mom's letters to me. I missed her so much. We got letters from her only three or four times while we were at Pulau Bidong, but those letters were very important. Things weren't going well back in Vietnam, but she didn't talk about those things because she didn't want to worry us.

In the Bataan camp, I went to school five hours a day, five days a week. School in the Philippines was more challenging than at Pulau Bidong, and

Binh Le (far left) with his little sister and brother at Bataan, Philippines, 1987.

there were more appropriate courses. At Pulau Bidong, we studied only English and math, and the classes lasted only an hour a day. The teachers on Bataan were Filipino and American instead of Vietnamese. In every class and every session, I won awards. In fact, I won academic awards at both Pulau Bidong and Bataan.

The main difference between our time in Malaysia and our time in the Philippines was that the native population associated with us in Bataan. It was more free and open than in Pulau Bidong. We also got more food in the Philippines, especially more fish. Also, in Muslim Pulau Bidong, pork was forbidden. They could beat you to death if they caught you eating it. I missed having pork so much. Three years without pork is a long time when you've been used to having it. When we got to the Philippines and were given pork, it was the greatest thing. We would either boil it or fry it on an oil stove they gave us.

At Bataan there were a lot of people from different charities. There were two Catholic churches at Bataan, and again I joined the youth group. One of the things this group did was study religion.

Here we also had cultural lessons to prepare us for America. Some things surprised me, such as gestures that meant "don't do this" or "don't do that." The time in Bataan seemed short because we knew for sure that we were going to America and could relax and focus on school.

Every day the camp officials would post announcements on the bulletin board to tell us where to go for interviews and paperwork. The posting was two weeks in advance so that we would know to prepare. Also, when we got letters, they posted that information on the bulletin board, so we had to check every day.

When we first found our name on a list for interviews, we were very happy, but then our emotions shifted from happiness to sorrow because we were leaving our friends. When we found out when we were leaving, we gave ourselves a tea party and invited our friends. We gave away all our things at our party—old clothes, pots and pans, utensils, blankets, even the garden where we grew vegetables. Then we just took a few clothes and went to the Manila airport by bus, and once again, I had to face motion sickness.

Manila wasn't very clean. It was dusty, chaotic, and frightening. People would just run into you. We waited at the Manila airport for a few hours, then left for Seattle, where we switched to another plane and flew to Memphis. The first two weeks in Memphis I was too terrified to leave the house, but eventually I got out into my new world.

You must be wondering what happened to my mother. When we left Vung Tau, I never thought I would see her again. It was very hard to

Binh Le with his sister, Tuyet, and friends in Memphis in 1997, when he and she became U.S. citizens.

leave. I knew we had a high chance of getting caught by the Communists. I missed my mom so much, and I would pray for her. I would say: "God, let me see my mom again. I will listen to her and not talk back to her and be a good child." I promised everything. Finally, in 1989, after we had been in Memphis for two years, the owner of a boat in Vietnam wrote us and asked us to pay for the passage of my mother and one brother. We couldn't believe it at first. We thought someone was trying to trick us into sending $3,000 in American money, and that was just half the price. My mom had already paid the other half. Then, in a few days, we received her letter, and she was in Pulau Bidong. Then we sent the boat owner the $3,000 we had saved.

My mom was on the last boat they accepted at Pulau Bidong. She stayed there two years, but she did not have to go to Bataan as we had. Instead she came straight to America because she had relatives here—us. When she arrived in Memphis, she started crying because she was so happy to see us. I stayed around her for days. I couldn't leave her. I hadn't seen her for seven long years—from 1984 until 1991.

I have two brothers still living in Vietnam. They did not leave at first because they had no money. Then they were too old and had their own families. We are in contact with them by letters, and sometimes we talk to them on the phone. Someday I'd like to go back and visit them. I haven't seen them for 13 years.

Chapter 11

Hainan, Hong Kong, and Tuen Mun Camp

Chau Nguyen was a student at Christian Brothers University at the time of this writing, majoring in Information Technology Management (ITM). He likes to read poetry, solve math problems, and play ping-pong and volleyball. Chau is active in the Memphis Buddhist Association.

When I was about 12, my father told me, "You better leave the country if you want to live." He was talking about the requirement that every male in Vietnam at age 18 must sign up for the military. If you don't go, they will hunt you everywhere. When he said this, I was scared. I didn't want to leave the country at all. Our family wasn't poor. We were in good shape, but my dad was afraid for me. He said, "You'd better either leave the country or cut off your finger." The reason some cut off their index finger was so that they couldn't shoot a gun and wouldn't then be forced into the military.

Not long after, my dad asked, "Are you going to leave, Chau?" I said: "No, Dad, you leave. I'll stay home alone." I said: "Just go. You can go with Mom. I want to stay home." I knew my grandparents were there. My uncles were there. I could live with them. Of course, I was very young and didn't know anything.

My family lived in Thon in the country near Hue City. It was so safe in Thon that sometimes I would sleep on the beach at night.

My father was a labor contractor for fishing boats. He hired workers to go out on boats; they fished for squid, sailfish, octopus, and shrimp, depending on the season. So you see, my father's reason for leaving wasn't economic.

99

About 5:00 one Sunday morning in the summer of 1988, my dad woke me up and said, "Chau, you need to go somewhere." I said, "Where?" Then he said: "I'm going to send you with some people. You're going to leave the country." Then he handed me some food, clothes, and a raincoat. I still remember the raincoat he wrapped around the rice, sugar, and some fish. Then we went to one of my relative's boats. My dad and I acted as if we were in this boat's crew and were going out for regular fishing.

You had to be very secretive. If the military found that you were planning to escape or caught you trying to escape, then they would arrest you immediately and punish you harshly. I knew a story about this married guy with five or six children who tried to leave the country four times. He would attempt to skip the country, get caught, and serve several years in prison. Each time he would come back home and try to escape again. His whole life was just serving time in prison, returning, planning another escape, and getting caught.

After my relative's boat had gone out for about three hours, we met another boat that was going to be the one I would escape on. It was a bigger boat, like a canoe with a deck and an engine. In this boat there were three men, all strangers to me. First I met them. Then I crossed over to the other boat, but when I crossed over, I had a long face. I was so scared. I told my dad I didn't want to leave, but he said, "You better go ahead and do it."

Then another boat came up with three brothers in it. As one of these men stepped on the bigger boat, he was crying because he said he didn't want to leave the country. His two brothers were saying to him, "Your wife and children are at home." Then he crossed back to his brothers' boat. For a while he had one foot in his boat and one foot in the larger boat. They were all crying and talking. Eventually they agreed that the two brothers would go first, and the third, with a wife and children at home, would come on another trip. They would send back information to him about when it would be good to go. So he went back to his wife and children.

Finally, my father said goodbye to me. I was so sad. I hadn't even had a chance to say goodbye to my mother before I left home, and I didn't know the men on the boat.

Soon we left, headed for Hainan, an island off the coast of southern China. In the daytime the men depended on the compass. They tied a rope from the head of the boat to the end of the boat. They looked at the compass needle to go north. The ride that afternoon was rough. It was the first time in my life I had been in such rough weather. It started raining. The turbulence made the waves high. I held on very tight to keep from being thrown out. Water was getting in the boat, and some of the men bailed it out with little baskets with wooden handles. There was no pump. The storm lasted for six or seven hours.

I was afraid I was going to be seasick because I had never been out so long or so far before. By this time we were well into the South China Sea. It was so dark—black. I couldn't see any stars or the moon. I just lay there that night, thinking about my parents and my sisters and brothers. What would I do in a place where I had no relatives? I would have nowhere to turn. Even though I didn't know these men, I knew I had to stick to them like sticky rice. I was so sad and afraid. I just lay there on the boat while the rest of them were busy doing all the steering and thinking about how to get to Hainan. I didn't speak to anyone.

Finally it was daylight, and the ocean was smooth. I looked around. That morning there was no one around us, just us alone on the ocean. Then we saw mountains and then houses and palm trees, but as we approached the people there shot at us. So we turned and ran away from there. It was a small island close to China. We could hear them shouting at us in Chinese.

By this time we were running low on fuel. We got to Hainan at about 8:00 or 9:00 at night. The Hainan harbor was very dangerous because it was full of many large ships. Even if you showed them a light to let them know where you were, you were afraid they were going to run over you. If they ran over you, they might not even know they had done it because they were so tall. They were like giants, and we were like a tiny dog. After the men moored our boat, I stepped onto the dock, but felt like I was still on the boat, rocking up and down. My whole body kept bouncing up and down. I said: "Oh, no. What has happened to me?" At Hainan we saw another Vietnamese boat that had arrived a few days earlier and had already settled in. This boat had not only men but also women and small children. When we eventually left the Hainan harbor, this boat and ours left together.

Soon after we arrived, the Chinese officials asked us why we had come there. To them, we were intruders. They were suspicious that we might be invaders, so they checked to see if we had guns or ammunition. They searched us and the boat. They didn't give us any food at all. I had no food until noon the next day. The men on our boat said I had to beg for food. But I said, "I'm not going to beg for food."

The men had some money, so they bought some rice and cooked it. They had only about three cups of rice, and there were no plates, so they poured it on a plastic bag. I still remember that all I got was six spoons of rice with salt for the whole day. It wasn't that good, but at least it was food. There were some poor people on Hainan who begged for food, but

I wouldn't beg. However, when I got to know some people from other boats, they gave me some food.

We stayed on Hainan a few days. During the second day, some of the men paid to send a radio message to my parents about the boat arriving in Hainan. The message contained the name of the owner of the boat so that my parents would know.

After three days we prepared to leave early in the morning. The men bought some fuel in plastic containers, and we left with the other boat that had arrived in Hainan before us. We thought it would be safer to travel together. After about six hours on the sea, a Chinese Navy boat stopped us. After they searched us and didn't find anything, they gave us fuel and rice and let us go.

The trip from Hainan to Hong Kong is deadly, utterly deadly. The trip from Vietnam to Hong Kong took one month and three days. It is easy to be killed by the weather because you are exposed to the sun and the rain. You could get the flu or pneumonia, and we didn't have any medicine. We would travel in the morning and stop about 6:00 or 7:00 so that we could see to cook. Then we would stop in the night and rest. Sometimes I would be on the other people's boat and sometimes on ours.

I felt alone and sad and very hungry. The clothes I wore were wet because it rained so much. I slept all the time. Sometimes when I slept, it was cold even though it was summertime. I was dirty and didn't have any blanket.

As we went along the Chinese coast, sometimes we would stop at a town, and if the weather wasn't too good, we would stay there one or two days. There is a short way to go to Hong Kong that takes only about seven days. But we didn't dare go that way because there is no one to help you that way. We would have had to go too far out in the ocean, and we didn't dare go that far out. It was too easy to die out there. The long way was safer.

We went in to the land many times, but I don't remember any of the names of the places because they were in Chinese. Most of the time we would sleep on the shore when we landed. In some hamlets, the government would let us stay in some small buildings because they were afraid we would scavenge around and disturb the people. But these buildings were more like prisons. They had dirty cement floors and usually smelled bad. One place smelled so bad I couldn't stand to stay in it. I tried to get out, but when I tried I found out that I was locked in. But they did give us food to eat.

One night when we landed we thought there would be people and houses, but there wasn't anyone, only trees. We didn't have any fresh water to cook the rice, so we used the salty ocean water. Have you ever tasted rice cooked like that in your life? No way can you eat it. It's just like eating salt. The rice was ruined, but we were lucky to have some potatoes that were left in the boat. That night we set up a tent from a tablecloth that was on the boat. We had no house, no water to drink, nothing. We were scared to death. We didn't know what might happen. In the morning we left.

Some days the weather was bad; we would just stay in the same place until the weather was better. Whenever we stayed on shore, we would learn from the Chinese people we met. We didn't know how to talk with them, but they would show us how to talk and how to count. I learned to count to ten in Chinese. One night we stayed in a place where the people cooked a lot of rice for us and gave us a lot of fish to eat. We even stayed in a house there.

Early the next day we left that place and arrived in Macau. The government people there asked us questions but didn't let us off the boat. They tied our boat to theirs, and we thought they were going to pull us from Macau to Hong Kong. But halfway there, they stopped and pointed us toward Hong Kong. They wanted us to go to Hong Kong on our own, and we wanted them to take us there. The owner of our boat pretended the engine was dead. So someone from the Chinese boat came on board and tried to crank it, but he didn't know how to operate it. So our boat owner said: "Oh, the engine's dead. We are trapped." They took us back to Macau, and there a Vietnamese translator explained that Macau Navy boats couldn't cross the marine border into Hong Kong because Macau belonged to China and Hong Kong to Britain. That is why we had to go by ourselves. Once we were there, the Hong Kong government would pick us up.

So again they led us, gave us some food, and we were on our way. When we arrived in the islands of Hong Kong in 1988, it was 9:00 or 10:00 at night, and some government boats picked us up. Of course, first they searched us and our boat. Then they took us to a special camp, where we stayed for a week. Here they took our fingerprints and filled out papers. At this camp they gave us some biscuits and canned food. I had never eaten canned food before. It was some kind of fish, but the fish made me want to vomit. It seemed rotten. I had eaten only fresh fish. I thought, "Oh, I have to eat this?"

At this camp there was no bed at all. Instead, they had some kind of mats for us to sleep on. The North Vietnamese were on one side of the building and the South Vietnamese were on the other, with only a space between, no wall. There was an imaginary line between us that we didn't cross. Even though they were Vietnamese like us, they spoke differently and were hard to understand.

When it was time to leave the first camp, they took us on a navy boat to the next. Here we were put into dorms. There were plywood beds stacked three high with nothing on the boards. They gave us a pair of pants, a shirt, a pair of underwear, a toothbrush and some toothpaste, a pair of slippers, a spoon, and a cup. I didn't know anyone at this camp except those from my boat. I didn't sleep with them, but I still ate with them.

Every day we had to stand in long lines to get food. Thousands of people were in the camp. We had to go early to get in line, and if you had to leave the line, you put a rock to hold your place, and people would honor it. They had different food for every day of the week. For example, Monday was cucumber soup and one chicken breast and rice. We had two meals a day.

While I was there I learned how to write a letter to my parents. I had paper from the school we went to, but I didn't have any stamps or envelopes. So at first I would go to the people I used to be with on the boat and ask them for an envelope and a stamp. I didn't have any money or any relatives to send me any money. Later when I wrote a letter to my parents, I would get an envelope and take it to a Buddhist monk, who would get a stamp and mail it for me. But I didn't get any letters from my parents yet. I wrote four letters, and I waited for an answer. When a letter for you finally arrived, a South Vietnamese guy would call out over the intercom, "Chau, boat 39, you have a letter." Every day at 5:00 P.M. you would listen to the intercom to find out if you had a letter waiting.

There were two main camps. If you went out of your camp to visit the other one, you had to be back by a certain time. When the count was taken each morning, if even one person was missing, all of us would have to wait to find out who was missing. If the count was not right, we had no lunch until it was correct. Every morning you had to go down while they counted. They didn't call your name. They just counted to see that the correct number of people were there.

I found out that I had a cousin who lived in the North Vietnamese camp. For some reason, a few South Vietnamese lived there. But when I visited him, I always got back plenty early. During the day, my cousin and I would play chess and soccer, watch television, and go to school. Then I would go back to the South camp.

The North side of the camp was by the water, but there was wire around it with sharp needles that cut. So I stayed away from the fence. One day someone passed the word that my cousin's parents had left Vietnam and that my dad had left too. When I heard this, I assumed my mother had left with him. Eventually my dad arrived at the camp, and I saw him through the fence. I also saw my two sisters and my brother, but I didn't see my mom. I said, "Where is my mom?" My dad said, "Your mom is staying home with the two youngest." My cousin's mom and my mom's sister had come, but not my mom.

When my dad arrived at the permanent camp, he started to work in the kitchen. By doing this, he was able to make some money. He also had access to food, which he could sell and make more money. When my dad came, life was much better for me. At that camp, people had a chance to go to work, but eventually we were transferred to another camp.

About three months after my dad came, we heard that my mom had left Vietnam. I had been in Hong Kong for almost a year when I heard that my mom had come. Meanwhile, we had moved to a camp where they prepared you to go into Hong Kong society and work there. This camp was to help you find a job and teach you how to support yourself. My dad got a good job making jeans, and he opened a savings account in Hong Kong. You could go out into the city, and they taught you how to get places.

While my dad was at work I had to go to school, like all other children under 18. We were bused to a school in Hong Kong run by Vietnamese who'd been in Hong Kong a long time.

When my mother came to Hong Kong, she was put in a different part of the camp because she was one of those who arrived after June 6, 1990. I finally got to see my mother and my sisters about one year and two months after I arrived in Hong Kong. We saw her at her small apartment. Mom had a job at a Styrofoam factory and was putting her earnings in the bank.

When my dad asked permission to have my mom join us, the camp officials wouldn't let her because our part of the camp was full. So we moved to Tuen Mun camp. We didn't really want to go there because it had people from the North. Sometimes the North people would beat us up. At first we wouldn't say anything. Finally, the South Vietnamese in Tuen Mun camp couldn't take the North Vietnamese anymore, so we decided to move out of the camp by illegally climbing over the fence. We stayed outside the fence on strike and said we wouldn't come in. The director of the camp said: "You can't do that. We won't let you eat." Finally we said, "We can't stay with those North people." The director said: "You go back first, and we will respond to you later. But we will respond to you one at a time, not all together." So we went back in humiliation, and those North people, they yelled and laughed. It was embarrassing, but they put us in a special building where we stayed with no North Vietnamese.

Chau Nguyen in Memphis, 1997.

I was in Hong Kong camps for two and a half years before we were moved to the Philippines. When we left Hong Kong, my dad withdrew all the money from the bank and bought a camera and clothes and many bags of noodles. We had about two weeks to prepare to leave for the Philippines. We knew that conditions there would be harsh.

It is true that the conditions in the Philippines were poor. There wasn't enough food, and the place wasn't clean. Water was turned off at 5:00 P.M., and lights were turned off at 10:00. But I did go to school where I studied math, English, social studies, and science. I was first in my class, and I still have the medals. We also learned how to behave in America and learned a lot about liberty.

Even though we are Buddhist, Catholic Charities ended up sponsoring us to go to the United States. It didn't matter if you weren't Catholic. I really wanted to leave the Philippines more than Hong Kong because it wasn't a good place. We had left Hong Kong in January 1990 and lived in the Philippines for seven months. We arrived in Memphis on July 1, 1990.

Chapter 12

Flight from Classification 13

Phung Le and his wife, Mai-Huynh Nguyen, settled in Memphis with five of their six children. They became United States citizens in 1995.

From 1962 to 1963, I was with the South Vietnamese Army at Thu Duc Military Training School, Bien Hoa Province. I graduated from Military Officers School in 1963. However, I left the army in 1966 to work as the clerk of the court in Vinh Long Province. After I earned a bachelor of laws degree at Saigon University in 1968, I rejoined the army, because of the Tet Offensive, as the division chief of litigation of military property for the Defense Department. I stayed in this position until the Communists took over the South in 1975. At the time of the fall, my wife, Mai-Huynh, and I had five children. After the Communist takeover, I was a prisoner in nine different reeducation camps over a period of nine years. Six of these years were spent in Hoang-Lien-Son Province, Yen Bai District, in the North and three in the South.

Many people who had been involved with the South Vietnamese government before April 30, 1975, were relocated to the New Economic Zones in virgin or unproductive areas. Conditions in these zones were generally acknowledged to be poor and were often life-threatening. The government continued to hold large numbers of people in such reeducation camps without trial or even charges. The purpose was to remove dissident elements and to produce conformity through hard labor and confinement.

Major Phung Le in Vietnam, 1973.

After my release from the reeducation camps, I was a so-called noncitizen and lived under strict surveillance. Each month I had to report my activities to the district police station. I couldn't leave my resident area of Thanh Phu District without permission. The authorities still considered me dangerous. I felt like a person at the bottom of society.

When I had been in the North, I saw an abandoned Catholic church and seminary that had been closed for so long that moss was growing on its walls. I also saw a Buddhist temple that had been closed, and I was told its leaders had been forced into reeducation camps. The Communists used the Buddhist temple as a depot for the collective farms. Private schools had been closed too. In addition, many teachers in the South had to undergo political indoctrination programs.

In addition to these problems, the country was suffering from hyperinflation that plunged most people into poverty. As a result, I lost any faith I might ever have had in the Communist Party.

If my children, now numbering six, had remained in Vietnam under these conditions, they would have continued suffering from discrimination. Under the Communists, people were classified from 1 to 14. In the best positions, the #1 positions, were the children of deceased Communist soldiers. These children were granted many benefits, such as priority status for attending university. My children were in position #13, reserved for the children of South Vietnamese military officers who had been in reeducation camps. The 14th position was reserved for traitors' children. As a result of this arrangement, my children would not have been qualified to attend college except as agriculture majors. I believed that the next three generations would have to endure the same deprivations. I knew that because I had no future and my children had no future, escape from Vietnam was the only hope.

The first time I failed to escape. My wife was put in jail in Truc Giang, Ben Tre Province, for six months. I managed to escape with my children and go to the home of my sister-in-law in Sa Dec Province. I was afraid they would put me in a reeducation camp again. My boat and my land were confiscated, and my house was torn down. The police moved the furniture from my house to the police station.

When my wife was released from prison, she came to Sa Dec and we took the children to my relatives in Thanh Phu District. We had nothing. I went to Saigon for about six months, then to Bao Loc, Da Lat Province, where I worked on a coffee plantation. In 1986, I went back to Saigon to look for someone to help me make plans for a second escape attempt. It was not easy. After our failed attempt, I knew I must be vigilant. I told myself, "We must look ahead, not back." My friend in Saigon told me the second attempt would take place three or four months after the lunar new year.

This journey was set up by a Vietnamese-Chinese who planned to escape with us. We had a secret meeting at my friend's house. I drew up the boat contract between the buyer and the seller. They got the boat at a local authority's auction. Oddly enough, this large boat had been used to hunt for escaping boats and to control the coast. We agreed to pay $3,000 for the boat when we arrived in America.

After that we made an appointment at the western bus station to go to the Can Tho ferryboat. After night fell, we crossed the Mekong River to the boat. It was moored only about 500 yards from the Tra Noc (Can Tho) navy base. We waited on the boat for 24 hours. The next night a lot of people poured onto our boat. They looked like disorderly, withdrawing troops. By this time there were 154 of us on board. At midnight our boat started toward Long Xuyen Province. We were looking for a canal that would lead into an estuary that went into the sea. It would be a more secret way out. We traveled by this canal to Rach Gia Province.

The boat crossed in front of a coastal defense station and got out into the estuary by midday and into Rach Gia Bay. About five miles from land, the boat slowed down, and I went up on deck to see what was happening. A Communist ensign who had taken a bribe from the boat owner to guide us out of the estuary was being picked up by a fishing boat to be taken to land. I saw that our boat had been flying the Communist flag. When the ensign left, we threw away our camouflage.

As I stood on the deck, I saw nothing but sky and water. The boat seemed to go only up and down, not forward. We needed a point of reference. At about 5:00 P.M. on that first day, we saw trees on a little island and could tell that the boat was moving forward. By this time, the people at the bottom of the boat were vomiting almost endlessly. When they weren't vomiting, they lay motionless, with only an occasional tear rolling down their cheeks from their unseeing eyes, pitiful and humble.

A half-hour before sunset, we saw another boat coming toward us. Our steersman changed direction to keep it from pursuing us.

On the way to Pulau Bidong, Malaysia, we saw three or four trading vessels, but they did not rescue us. We also saw two Thai fishing boats who made flashlight signals for us to stop our boat. However, when we stopped they did not board our boat or rob us.

On the third day, two terrible thunderstorms hit us, each lasting about an hour. Our boat was dashed by the big waves that seemed to be trying to destroy it. Everybody prayed: "Lord, help us. Lord, save us." The second thunderstorm was over within an hour, and the boat was still running. An hour before sunset the steersman said to me, "We have no more oil for the engine." After the storms we didn't know if we were headed for the Thai or the Malaysian coast. He guessed that we would get to land by midnight, but at about 8:00 P.M. we saw a glimmering light far away. Our boat headed that way. The closer we got to the light, the happier we felt, the more sure we were that we would survive. We felt incredible joy.

To our horror we found out that the lamps were being used by fishermen to catch fish. When our steersman asked one of the men where Pulau Bidong was, the fisherman told us that he would tow us there for $2,000. By this time our boat had stopped running.

Because the fishermen wanted to fish all night, we had to wait until the next morning to leave. We were not so far from the land, and yet our motor still wouldn't start. We were finally towed by the fishing boat to Pulau Bidong, where all 154 of us arrived at about 5:00 P.M.

After our arrival in June 1986, I stayed there about two months. After two months the American delegation accepted me because I had been a major in the South Vietnamese military. I then went to Sungei Besi, Malaysia transit camp, and then to Bataan, Philippines, for six months. Catholic Charities sponsored me to come to the United States.

After I arrived in Memphis in May 1987, I filed a petition to have my wife and six children come to America. My wife, three sons, and two daughters arrived here in December 1992. A second daughter is married and still in Vietnam. We are trying to get her to America with her husband.

I now own my house in Memphis, and both my wife and I have jobs. Here our children can get good educations. I am happy living in America. Maybe someday my children will go back and visit our relatives in Vietnam.

Phung Le with his daughter Yen-Thanh Le in Memphis, 1997.

I hope that my children will get better jobs than my wife and I have. My oldest boy is a chemical technician at International Paper in Memphis. Four children still go to school: one to the University of Memphis, one to State Tech at Memphis, one to Richland Elementary, and one to a vocational school where he studies automotive mechanics. I have often told my children, "If you don't help yourself, nobody else will."

Chapter 13

I'd Rather Die in the Sea

Anton Vo graduated from the University of Buffalo, with a double major in chemistry and medicinal chemistry. He went on to a job in the pharmacokinetics department at a Memphis hospital.

One night in 1964 my mom and dad were sitting together eating dinner in their house in Nha Trang when two armed Communist men rushed into the house. They killed my father, but because my mom was pregnant, they decided not to kill her.

Three months later, in December 1964, my mother bore me, so I never saw my father, who had worked with the Americans as chief of Nha Trang. In 1967 my mother had a chance to get married again, and I went to live with my grandmother.

When I lived with my grandmother, I had to go to school and do things on my own. Nobody could help me at all. Eventually my grandmother decided to send me to a Catholic boarding school in Nha Trang. I began this school when I was five years old and came home to visit my grandmom only one or two days a month. During my years at the boarding school, I concentrated on my studies and, for the most part, played by myself.

When the Communists took over the country in 1975, the seminary closed, and I had to go home and stay with my grandmom. By then I was 11. But I continued going to school. When the time came to go to college, it was very hard for me to get in. Although I had passed the exams, because my father had not been a Communist, I was not accepted. But when I got a very high score the next year, they let me in. In college I majored in Vietnamese literature. But after graduation I couldn't get a decent job because my father had not been a Communist.

During both high school and college, I tried to escape from the country several times but couldn't make it. During the 11th grade I tried to escape by boat, but I got caught and they put me in jail for three months. They kept me for only three months during that summer because I was under 18. In prison they gave me two meals a day: a bowl of rice without anything else, and maybe a bowl of sauce with water. When my mom and my grandmom gave them money under the table, they let me out and I returned to school.

After I finished high school, I tried to escape again. That time I was 18 years old, so they put me in jail for one year. It was a sad situation, and again the same thing happened. My mom and my grandmom gave them money under the table, and they let me out. The summer after my first year in college I tried to escape again, got caught again, and was put in jail for three months. Sometimes in prison they would beat me. They just wanted to get money from me. If you gave them money, everything was okay. If you didn't give them money, they beat you. The main thing is the money—nothing else.

Then I finished college and got a poor job teaching at Ly Tu Trong High School. After one year there, I tried to escape again. This time I made it. It was my fourth try.

I made this fourth attempt because I had no future in Vietnam. Even if you have money and a degree, you cannot do anything with your life. If you are a Communist, you can move on with your life. If you are not a Communist—never, never can you move ahead. So that is the reason I wanted to escape the country. I would rather die in the sea than live in Vietnam. Those of us who escaped had no choice. If you got lucky, you could go to another country and move on with your life. If you didn't make it, then you would rather die in the sea. That's why there were 42 people on the boat.

We all knew that if we worked together, we could collect the money we needed and buy a boat, and this we did. We escaped the country about 4:00 in the morning. Fortunately, Nha Trang is right on the coast. The day before the actual escape, five or six of us hid in a public toilet and waited for a signal, and then, at 4:00 A.M., we got the signal and ran right onto the boat. It took five minutes for all 42 of us to get on board.

We spent two weeks on the sea in an open boat. The first two days we were seasick, but after that we could stand up and look at the sky and the water. That was all you could see, just water and sky. There was one big storm, but we survived it. We had accepted death already. When we stepped onto the boat, we accepted death together.

After one week we ran out of water and out of food. So we fished and ate the fish raw. After ten days, the engine stopped working. After that we didn't know what we were going to do. We didn't see anybody until the 11th day, when a big ship stopped and gave us some water and canned food. They couldn't help us with our engine. On the 12th day, we saw three Filipino fishing boats. We signaled them to come over and told them we would give them money if they would pull us to land. They agreed, then pulled us close to an island, and we paddled to shore.

Anton Vo in 1978 in Nha Trang.

During our two weeks on the sea, two people died because they drank seawater. One was a man and one was a woman, not related. After they died, we threw them into the sea.

After we got to the land, we just lay down and slept. We were like dead bodies on the seashore. We heard that they took us to the hospital. After two days in the hospital, we were back to normal, and then we went to the refugee camp. There we met a lot of people who had come there before us.

At the Palawan Island refugee camp in the Philippines, they gave us enough food to eat and enough water to drink every day. We could take showers, and we had a place to sleep too. Actually, the time we lived there was happy because we knew for sure that we would never see the Communists again. But we still worried about our future.

The 40 of us from the boat who had survived were separated at the camp. About three weeks after we were settled in, we could go to school and learn English for one hour a week. Every day we all had to do some kind of work. Within a month, government officials from lots of countries—the United States, Canada, France, Australia, and others—had interviewed us for immigration.

My first interview was with the French government, but they didn't accept me. I was happy because I didn't want to go to France; I wanted to go to America. The second interview was with the American government, but they didn't accept me either. They told me to wait for a second interview with them. A year after the first interview with the Americans, I was called again, and this time they accepted me. I went through five rounds of interviews. Then one day in school I heard my number on the public-address system. They said those called were to go home and get dressed and prepare to go to Bataan, Philippines. We were to transfer to Bataan and later be transferred to America. Oh, man! I was so happy. I just swung by home, got everything ready, and left there around 2:00 P.M. by jet. That ended my three years—1988, 1989, and 1990—on Palawan Island.

Although I was happy to leave Palawan, I had many happy memories of my stay there. Once I learned my way around, I was able to help other people out. I helped people solve problems such as how to deal with homesickness and even with physical illnesses. At Palawan we had hope. There was a 60 or 70 percent chance that you could get to another country. You might not know what country—but you still had somewhere to go.

When I left Palawan, I took my first plane ride, and I thought it was fun. They took me to Manila—a very big city—and put me in a transition place. I slept one night there before being taken to the refugee camp by bus the next morning.

I lived in Bataan for one year. Most people were there for only six months, but I stayed longer because some paperwork was messed up. Even though there were a lot of Vietnamese on Bataan, they got along well because they were all in the same situation. Besides, there were also a lot of Amerasians.

Not long after I came to Bataan, I became a teacher's assistant. From 7:00 A.M. until noon, I was a student myself, learning more English. However, from 1:00 until 5:00 I translated Vietnamese into English for the teacher in the American culture class. I translated three days a week in the school and two days a week in the office where people were interviewed for their paperwork. On the weekends I worked for the church, and at night during the week I taught Vietnamese to the little kids.

Although my days and nights were busy, I was very happy because I knew that what I was learning would make me more comfortable when I got to America. I just had to take care of myself and learn the culture of the United States. When I left Bataan, I felt so sad because I had a lot of fun there and had a lot to do there. I worried about what I would do in America. Should I go to school and study there, or should I get a job?

When I came to America—to Buffalo, New York—I cried and cried because I could not speak English. I could not understand people's pronunciation, and they could not understand mine. I worried so about myself. I wondered how I could adapt to this country. I cried every day. But after one week, I said: "No. You can't cry anymore. You have to do something to prove to yourself you can survive. You have to go to school to learn English again." Every day, in Buffalo's snow and cold, I walked to class to study English. From my house to school was a 30-minute walk every day. I studied English from 8:00 A.M. to 2:00 P.M. After six months, I could do things for myself. Then I decided to go to the University of Buffalo and get a degree.

The first year of college I struggled. Because the teacher talked very fast, I used a tape recorder, and when I got home, I would listen to the tape and read more books. I worked very hard, and after one year in college, I had a good grade-point average. I felt so happy, even though my English was still not that good. I felt okay. I made friends with American people and hung around with them and tried more English. It was still hard because I had to work after school to get some money for myself, and sometimes I would send money to my mother and my grandmother in Vietnam too.

So it was like this every single year: just study and make some money. In 1996, after four years at the University of Buffalo, I graduated and got a job down here in Memphis, where it is warmer, and I feel very lucky.

Chapter 14

Coffee Shop
from Two Spoons

Hung Nguyen settled in Memphis with his wife, Thu Ha Vo.
During his early years in Memphis, he was the organist
and choir director of the Vietnamese congregation at Sacred
Heart Catholic Church. Later he took a job with Georgia
Pacific, where he worked as of this writing.

In Vietnam my family was always very political. When my father was a
young man, he served as a translator for the French, and in 1963 he became
a lieutenant in the South Vietnamese Army. During his time as an officer,
he was the head of Bien Hoa. My oldest brother was a heart surgeon who
worked for the United States government. My younger brother also
worked for the Americans, and my oldest sister worked for the United
States Embassy.

My family's close connection with the U.S. government became a
major problem after the Communists took over in 1975. Both my oldest
and my youngest brothers were put in reeducation camps. My oldest
brother, who was in for four years, was lucky because he was in a Southern instead of a Northern camp. In the Southern camp he was able to do
a little work to feed himself. My youngest brother stayed in a reeducation
camp for only one year. Because my father was older, the Communists
didn't touch him.

When my father left the South Vietnamese Army in 1975, he started
a chicken farm. The chicken farm grew so fast that it was the biggest in
our city of Can Tho, which is about 100 miles south of Saigon on the Cuu

Long delta. Everyone knew my father because he sold so many chickens every day and the farm was big. Besides the chickens, he also raised pigs.

But when the Communists took over, they said the farm was too big for my father to handle, so they took most of it away. They let him have what they called "enough," based on how many people were in the family. So my father continued to be a chicken farmer but on a smaller scale. Between 1975 and 1977, he decided to sell all the things he had to collect money to buy a boat and get out of Vietnam. But even with all the money he gathered, he still did not have enough to buy the boat, the gas, or an engine, the basic things. He had to look for people he could trust so that he and they could put their money together and escape. My father could not actually sell the land. All he could do was sell the chickens and the equipment and even take down a few walls and sell them piece by piece.

Within a year we bought a boat, but we couldn't furnish it. It was not a long, narrow river boat but a short, wide carry boat that was much bigger. A carry boat transports things from one city to the next. Even though this kind of boat is not made to go out into the seas, we didn't care. We just wanted to get out of the country as fast as we could.

It took two years to plan the escape. Eventually we completed the boat and made our first escape attempt. We tried to pick up people from various places to make sure no one was watching us, but we messed up on the timing and failed. No one got caught.

After this first attempt we had another problem. The engine broke down because we tried to run it at maximum power. We were trying to see how long the engine could stay at that maximum power. When we tried to rebuild the engine, we ran out of money again. But before long we had collected enough money again. Luckily, we found someone to rebuild the engine, and we tried a second escape.

The second time was a success. We picked up people like we were supposed to. Plus we had come up with the idea of reducing the noise of the engine to keep it from sounding like a three-block engine. We made a muffler to reduce the noise so that the Communists would not recognize it as a big boat trying to get out of the country.

We took two guns with us, including a Colt .45. The guns were for us to use as a signal in case the police saw our boat. "Boom, boom, boom" was to be the answering signal to the police. If we knew how to answer their signal, then they would believe we were friends.

There were 34 people in the boat. From my family there were my mom and my dad, my aunt, my parents' seven children including me, as well as my wife and my sister-in-law. I was 26 years old when we escaped in December 1979.

On the night we escaped, December 15, 1979, the water level was so low that we couldn't make much progress. We started at Can Tho but got stuck. We had to use a long pole to get the boat out. After we got unstuck, it took us two hours to get down the river and into the South China Sea. About an hour later everyone got seasick. The waves were ten times higher than the boat, and the farther we got out on the sea, the bigger the waves were. Suddenly the waves started to go crazy, and the boat tipped over. Everyone was scared. Two waves slammed the front and the back of the boat. Fortunately, the waves had cracked the boat only on the top, not on the bottom. But we all had to bail water out because the pump had worn out. My brother had a compass that showed we were headed for Taiwan, but my mom was so seasick she asked my brother to try to go back toward Thailand instead because it was nearer. This change helped because the wind and waves were going in the direction of Thailand anyway.

My wife was seasick the worst. Plus she was homesick for all the family she had left behind in Can Tho. All she had was me and my family.

It took us four days to reach Thailand. We knew we were near Thailand when my brother heard the forecast from Bangkok on his little radio. At that time, we were running at half-speed, and everybody felt good. We all forgot about the engine and went on top to look around at the dolphins and big fish. We had so much fun watching the dolphins swim along with us.

Then the engine quit; it had locked up. I had to open up the engine to see what was wrong. First we found that the bearings were messed up. I opened up the connecting rod and tried to remove the worn-out bearings. At the moment I picked up the bearings I only half believed in God, but I said, "God, let these become the original bearings so the engine can run again." I asked everyone to pray to God that these bearings would become the original ones. Then we put the engine together again, only now we found that we had no oil left. All we had was two pounds of bearing grease that we used to grease the shaft that turned the propeller. We mixed the bearing grease with the gasoline to make oil. We poured the grease into the engine and then tried to crank it. I decided to have four people to assist in the cranking—two in the front of the engine and two in the back. It took four people because we were so weak. We hadn't eaten in several days, so my brother suggested that each of the four eat one lemon by just putting it in our mouths and trying to chew and swallow it. We did this for about 15 minutes and tried to relax. This way we were able to get enough power in our bodies. So the four of us tried to crank the engine again. It cranked. Everyone was so happy. But we forgot to thank God.

The oil pressure went down again in the next five minutes, so I had to sit down again to figure out what was wrong. The gasoline in our mixture had evaporated. This time we had no oil and no grease, but we had animal fat in a gallon can for cooking. After I mixed this with gasoline to make it become oil, the engine cranked again and everyone was happy. We got enough oil pressure so that we could go. One person watched the oil gauge all the time, even though the gauge was right in front of the guy running the boat. We still wanted someone whose only job was to watch the oil gauge. The engine oil smelled so good it made everyone hungry. It smelled like food cooking, but we had no food, only water.

Three or four hours later we saw a great-big fishing boat. I'd never seen one so big in my life. Then more came. Suddenly they all started following us, about 15 or 20 of them. We put on full power. As we came closer to the coast, we saw smaller fishing boats. They tried to stop us by surrounding us. We pulled a gun out and shot toward them. They backed off a little bit, but then they came on again. One of the boats hit the back of our boat and tore off a little of the back end. Our engine was still going the maximum speed. Then they pulled out what looked like a little BB gun and tried to shoot us. We weren't scared. We would just stand there and fight if we had to. Then we came up with an idea to slow them down. We dropped an empty 20-gallon gasoline can over the side, hoping they'd think it was a bomb. They did slow down to pick up the can, and when they saw that it was empty, they came back to within 20 feet of us.

Then my mom and dad wanted to try something else. My parents raised up a 12-inch cross that looked like gold. My mom also held up a picture of the Virgin Mary, with the idea that the power of God would save us. The longer they raised up the cross and the picture, the closer the boats got, the men thinking the cross was gold. Later on when we got to the land, they told us this. As we got closer to the shore, the larger boats left, and smaller boats that looked like canoes got closer. The men on board had long knives and axes and hammers, and they waved them in the air at us. We continued to run the engine at full power, and the engine was making a noise, louder and louder. We couldn't escape them. They got on our boat and fought us, trying to take everything we had. In the next 20 minutes, the whole boat was torn up good. Then they hooked a big chain to our boat and pulled it out of the sea with a tractor.

Despite all that happened, all 34 of us survived. We were all hit, but not hurt a lot. My mother was cut on the finger because she didn't want to pull off her ring. They used a knife to cut her finger to scare her, but they didn't cut the finger off. My mother was the only one who was cut.

The pirates had already taken everything that we had, any gold and

Hung Nguyen and his wife Thu Ha Vo (second and third from right, second row) with Hung's brother Cuong (far right on second row) and those who escaped in the boat together, February 1980.

watches, and now they wanted the boat and the engine. Then the head of the community took us to his home. It was a big house with a big front porch. We found out later, after someone parked the tractor beside his house, that he was in charge of the people who had robbed us of everything, including the boat. All my wife and I had left were the shirt and pair of shorts we each wore.

But after this man got our boat, he did help us. He knew we were hungry, so he cooked dinner for us. We weren't sure what the food was, but there was a lot of it, and we were very hungry. After we ate, the head man passed out cigarettes to the men. Everyone sat on the porch and enjoyed smoking cigarettes. We knew we had lost everything, and we accepted that.

About 45 minutes later, the Red Cross from Thailand arrived in a minivan. There were about four Red Cross representatives. One of them carried a gun and looked like a security guard. The Red Cross representatives made us stand in a line to check us out. They made us strip completely to do a body search. They checked to see if we had some more gold hidden in our clothes. They took the women to a room and stripped and searched them also to make sure they hadn't hidden anything in their underwear. So we ended up completely emptyhanded. About an hour

Thu Ha Vo and Hung Nguyen (standing second and third from right) at Songkla, Thailand, one week before going to the Philippines, 1980.

after that, at 9:00 or 10:00 P.M., they brought a bus to transport us from the seashore to Songkla Refugee Camp. We left everything. We didn't look back. Our bodies were safe.

When we arrived at Songkla, the authorities asked us if we had been robbed, but we said no. We thought if we said yes, the Thai police officers might get mad because we had said something bad about their people. We said nothing about what had occurred in the last few hours.

The camp was very crowded. The first night we slept on the sand, but no one was really able to sleep because of the numbers of people arriving every minute, every hour. The next morning, supplies arrived. These supplies allowed two people to sleep on one 28-inch-wide blanket on the sand. We were housed in a tent with flaps. We waited two to three weeks before we were able to move up into the building where there were bunkbeds. We couldn't move into these buildings until those already in them were sent somewhere else in the world. The worst thing about Songkla was that they would run out of supplies, especially clothing. But we had enough food. To take a bath, we swam in the sea and then walked along the shore so that the wind would blow us dry. At first we had no change of clothes, but when people's names came up on the list to be transferred to other countries, they would give away their old clothes.

During the mornings, the camp authorities would open the gates for two hours for those who had money to go and do a little shopping. During that time I called everyone who had a little money rich, since I didn't have any. What I did was follow the rich people, and when they bought new shoes or new sandals, they would throw away the old ones. Then I would ask them if I could have their old shoes. That's how I came up with my good sandals. I told my wife to do the same thing, to follow a lady. The sandals I got were a little bigger than my feet, but that didn't hurt.

During the first three weeks it was very hard to adjust to life in the camp. One thing that helped was that the whole family was Catholic. We worshiped God and got involved with the Catholic community to try to forget what had happened. There were activities going on every day. I joined the choir at our little church and played the accordion that Father Joe borrowed from someone. When the man wanted his accordion back, I had nothing to play, so Father Joe obtained a harmonica for me. It was just a kid's harmonica, but I could play the hymn tune on it. This was about ten days before Christmastime, so everyone was very happy that we had something to make a tune with. We had a wonderful Christmas at the camp. Father Joe took a picture of us to show it outside so that we could get more help. Later on people from the outside sent us a guitar.

There was very little to do at the camp. The only time you'd go to the office was when they called you on the intercom to do paperwork. Other than that, you had the whole day free. So we really had fun at the refugee camp practicing songs every day. But it wasn't long, about two months, before our paperwork was complete and they transferred us to the Philippines.

When we first arrived at Bataan, it was about 2:00 A.M. It was cold because we were in the high mountains. We had no blankets, but we found cardboard cartons where we could lie down. Plus we found some newspapers to cover our bodies so that we could sleep that night. The next morning a Philippine officer directed us to the Processing Center to complete our paperwork. Then we were assigned to a house. Each house was divided into ten units. Each unit had six people, no matter if you were single. My wife and I wound up with a family of four: mom and dad and two children. So there were two families in this one unit. You had to have two people on one blanket, and when my wife and I got one blanket, we were so happy. Each unit got one cooking stove and two pots. So my wife and I got one pot, and we took turns with the other family using the stove.

The buildings where we stayed had only a roof and two sides, with no front or back walls. The building contractors were way behind schedule.

The next day several old people with knowledge looked down the mountain at a lot of bamboo trees. They got the idea that we should go down and cut some of this bamboo to make curtains to cover the front and back ends of the building. We got about 40 men together to do this work. We tore the bamboo trees down with stones, since we did not have knives or axes. Then we carried them back to the buildings, and one of the workers for the contractors saw what we were doing and let us borrow some axes. We took all day building these bamboo walls to block out the wind. The bamboo walls stood for one month before the contractors came back and put up permanent walls.

The worst thing was that we had no water supplies. Once a day a two-wheeled U.S. Army water truck brought in what looked like a 100-gallon tank. Each of us stood in line for only a two-gallon bucket of water. We would quickly run out. Downhill there was a stream, and we asked permission to walk down there to get water. At first they wouldn't let us go because they were afraid wild animals would attack us, but we went anyway. During that time, the U.S. government had a contract to build a pump to bring water from the stream back to the Processing Center. But it was not successful because the pump was not powerful enough to transfer water from a stream two miles away and so far up a steep hill. So to get more water, we had to go down the hill and bring a bucket back up, and while we were down there, we'd take a bath.

Meanwhile we didn't have any restrooms either. We had to go to the woods. Then the contractors finished some restroom buildings. They were able to pump water to these buildings only once a day, from 10:00 A.M. to noon. The way they built these restrooms was funny. Each was one long building divided into rooms, and a gutter ran the length of the building through each room. During the two-hour period when the water pumps were working, the gutters could be flushed when the attached buckets were filled with water and overflowed into the gutters. To use the restroom, you had to straddle the gutter. There was no paper, so you had to wipe your bottom with your hand. There were faucets for washing your hands, but these had water only during the same two-hour period. From noon one day until 10:00 A.M. the next day is a long time to go without water to flush the gutters or wash your hands. So the gutters would get filled up. It smelled terrible. The first day these buildings were opened, the system worked, but the second day they had to lock the buildings up because too much tried to go down the chute at one time. Plus the people would try to find anything they could to wipe their bottoms, and this material would also clog up the chute. I don't know how in the world they came up with that system. Even though they made some improvements,

Hung and Thu Ha Nguyen at camp in Bataan, 1980.

the system did not work, and the people continued to use the woods for a restroom.

During the daytime in the Bataan camp, the U.S. government got Filipinos to conduct English classes. The classes were divided by ages, and each person had to attend so many hours a day to show on their records. When the class was over, the instructor would verify how many hours you had attended. They gave us a test, but we didn't pass even though we had studied real hard. Even when the class time was over and the teacher had gone home, we stayed in the classroom to try to learn more.

People at the center came up with their own ways of making money. Some of them made bread and sold it. Filipinos set up a money exchange from their relatives all over the world, and this money had to be changed to pesos. We used the peso to buy stuff on the market when we could. Filipinos also brought in food to sell on the open market. People caught and sold all kinds of things, including fish, lizards, and alligators.

Just as in the Thai camp, we had a Catholic choir at Bataan. This one had about 60 members. Almost every Catholic teenager joined with us, even if they had never sung before. They joined because we seemed to be having fun. Again we had no equipment. Our old equipment at the Thai camp had belonged to Father Joe, and we could not take it with us when we left. But we asked a nun working in the camp if she could get us an instrument. Somehow she got in touch with a Vietnamese sister who had lived in the Philippines for a long time. Both of them got together and sat down to listen to what we needed. Within a month they came up with a guitar, and we practiced singing with that guitar.

Soon Easter was coming up. By this time our choir's reputation was so great that a Filipino bishop came to hear us. After he heard us, he invited us to sing at his church outside the camp on Easter, so we sang our Vietnamese songs at his church. The bishop furnished the bus and food supplies for us to travel the two hours to his city. We had so much fun. The bishop said he had announced our coming and had never had that many people attend before. It was a huge crowd. Before long back at the camp it was Pentecost season, and here came the bishop with ten priests who traveled with him to the Processing Center. After we welcomed him to the center, we directed him to our little church, where everyone had already gathered for Mass. Right behind the bishop they carried a harmonium with a red ribbon around it. We took off the ribbon and put the harmonium at one side of the altar. The choir stood on the other side. This harmonium had a keyboard and pedals to pump the air in, and I began to play away. I had never played a harmonium before, but I did that day. Our nun was happy because we had jumped right in and played it and sang with it. We had a big celebration right there. About a week later we received a microphone and amplifiers from this bishop and his group of priests. Then I became the assistant choir director and continued to play the harmonium.

This bishop did something else very good that wound up helping the whole camp. Everyone in the Processing Center wore all different kinds of clothes. This didn't look too good when the people in the choir got together to sing. The bishop didn't like this, so he ordered blue jeans and white shirts for all the choir members to use when we sang for him. These clothes made us look better than everyone else. Soon some people started to complain and ask why we were so special, why we had such good clothes. Within a couple of weeks the U.S. government jumped in. Soon everyone 17 years old and older was eligible to receive one pair of blue jeans and one white shirt. Now everybody was happy. We wore these clothes to church every Sunday. Most of us didn't have shoes or sandals, but we all had white shirts and blue jeans.

Meanwhile months went by and more and more people arrived at the camp and more buildings went up. During this time of great expansion, I started running a little coffee shop, even though I didn't have money. Some refugees had opened the coffee shop, probably with money sent by relatives from around the world. But my family had no relatives in that position. About two months after the shop opened, the person who had operated it was transferred to the United States. Before he left, he transferred everything into my brother's name. My brother ran the shop for one month before he went to the United States. Before he left, he transferred the shop to me for the same amount of money that he had paid—$50. I told my brother I would pay him when I got to the United States. I operated the shop for two months and then received my transfer to the United States. I then sold the shop to the next person on the list for the same amount with the same agreement. I gave him information regarding where I would be in the States. That person did look me up here and paid me.

The coffee shop was very simple. It was against one end of the ten-unit building where I lived. It had an awning and tables. The tables were made from scrap wood and scrap nails that we collected from the construction site. The tables were basically junk, but they worked. We used a sheet or anything that looked nice and clean to cover the tables. We got our cups and saucers from a Filipino who also supplied us with coffee, Coke, and cigarettes. He agreed that he would give us supplies, and we would pay him the next time he stopped by. It was all based on trust. The Filipinos here were very nice to us. They found we could run the business, so they gave us their own money for the investment. At that time all the coffee shop inventory cost $15–20. We repaid him $5-10 each time until we finally paid off everything. By the time I sold it, the shop could have as many as 50 customers at once. One 16-inch square table could seat four to six people. When I look back at it now, I know it looked funny. Also, when I look back, I realize that I cheated on electricity, but I didn't realize it at the time. We used the electricity from the main building, since there were no sockets for us to use. I made a heat element from two spoons to heat the water for the coffee.

During the time I worked with the choir, I also ran the coffee shop. The sister would bring visitors to my shop and introduce me as the best musician. At my shop I received lots of music books written in English and Filipino. The coffee shop soon had so many customers that the sister stopped me one day and said, "Hung, you've got to spend your time with the church and not so much with the coffee shop." So I cut back on my business and did whatever the church needed me to do.

But we kept the harmonium at the coffee shop so that whenever there was free time we could practice the songs for the next Sunday. We had a big conference room we could use to practice our songs. One time I got a complaint that I was using the music to entertain at my coffee shop, so I cut it out. I think some people got jealous because my coffee shop got bigger. It also seemed like every time a group of people came to visit the camp, they would come by and visit the coffee shop.

From the coffee shop I made about $100, and I used that $100 to come to the United States. We knew $100 wouldn't mean much in the United States, so we spent it carefully.

When we escaped from Vietnam, my family was all together, but when we arrived in Songkla, Thailand, the United States government divided us into three separate groups—my brother and his wife, me and my wife, and my parents and my single brothers and sisters. When we came to Bataan, my brother's application was approved first because his wife already had a brother in Memphis. My mother and father went next, and my wife and I were the last to go. When they interviewed me again to find out whether I knew anyone already in the United States, I told them about my married brother and my parents and other siblings in Memphis. Then they said my wife and I could come to Memphis. I didn't even know where Memphis was or anything about it.

When we received approval to go to the States, we had to return all the things that had been loaned to us, such as the stove, blankets, and pots, in good order on the day before we left. The next day everyone got together to leave for Bangkok. We stayed at a center in Bangkok for one day to wait for our plane. The place where we stayed looked like a big parking garage. You'd just lay your sheet down and sleep on the floor. The next day we left for the United States and arrived in Memphis on October 29, 1980.

In 1995, my wife and I returned to our hometown of Can Tho. The main reason we went was to see my wife's family. We had been away from the country for 15 years. Almost all of my wife's family were back in Vietnam, and some of them wrote us and said they were eager for us to come. I had only uncles and aunts left there. Several things made it easy for us to visit at this time. My wife could take a leave of absence from her work whenever she wanted. I had been working for a railway company for three years but had been laid off, freeing me to go—except for one thing. I had a business on the side, a self-service coin-operated laundry in two different locations in West Memphis, Arkansas. Fortunately, one of my wife's cousins who had been here three years knew enough English to take over for me for one month. So we spent an entire month in Can Tho.

Among the Vietnamese, when you marry someone, you marry that person's whole family. I saw my wife's family as my own. Her parents had died, and now the oldest child, my wife's oldest sister, was in charge of the other brothers and sisters until they married. As long as they are still single, they depend on that person very much. It is a big responsibility. My wife and I over the years began to see ourselves as their parents. That

Hung Nguyen's family at the celebration of his parents' 55th wedding anniversary in Memphis, 1996.

is what made us go. We felt that we must send them money and take care of them just like they were our own children.

We spent almost $20,000 to go back to Vietnam in 1995, but we didn't think we had lost that money. We knew our family needed us to restore their love, their memory, because their brother and sister had been away so long. It helped them mentally, not just financially.

When we compared what they had in Vietnam with what we had here in the United States, it looked like hell and heaven. That is why we don't mind helping them out, then or now. When I talk to people in the United States about this, they don't understand why we do this. It's because I have a responsibility to them. They aren't like in-laws; they are like brothers and sisters and maybe even more like our children.

It's a funny thing about my wife and me not having children. When we married in 1977, we wanted to wait to have children because things were so bad. Then we escaped and wound up in terrible places, Songkla and then Bataan, so again we didn't want to have children. When we came to the United States, we struggled with our lives every day—studying English, trying to get a better job. Then we didn't want any children. Our hands were so full. Finally, I got a good job as an aircraft mechanic with West Memphis Jet Center, and we had enough money to have children, but then we found out that we couldn't have children. We both went to doctors for five years and spent lots of money, but nothing worked. We finally decided that maybe nothing was wrong with us. Maybe God planned it that way. Not having children gave us the time and money to support the brothers and sisters and nieces and nephews in Vietnam. So we accepted the fact that we have no children of our own and are happy with things this way.

These relatives back in Vietnam are now in the process of completing their paperwork. My wife and I have already completed our support paperwork, the form 134, which questions whether we have a good job, what our income is, and how much money we have in the bank. We had to complete our paperwork before they could qualify to come over. Even if we lose everything, we will still be happy.

Eventually 22 relatives will be living here with me and my wife. Each of them should be with us in about 14 months. That's our plan. We can do it. I know we can. Besides, I have a lot of people around me who will help me when the time comes. Those people know I am not a bad guy. They know I try to do my best for myself and my family. They can look at my life in the past and see that my situation now is 100 percent different. Based on that, they can trust me and are willing to help out. Help will come from my family, other Vietnamese, church groups—both Baptist and Catholic—and the government. All will help.

Note: Between August 1997 and February 1998, all 22 of the relatives from Vietnam came to Memphis. Two families have already bought their own houses, and two other families have houses under contract. The nine children in this group are all in school, six in elementary and three in high school.

Chapter 15

Coolie in America

Nhan T. Le settled with her husband in Manchester, New Hampshire. The couple has two children. As of this writing Nhan was working at an electronics company as a board tester. She enjoys reading Vietnamese novels and spending time with her family.

In a family of nine, five sisters and four brothers, I am the baby, a girl. I was born in the year of the water buffalo according to the Chinese zodiac. I didn't know what my fate would be. This is my story.

I was only 14 years old when the North invaded the South. I didn't know anything about politics. The only thing I knew was to study. After I finished high school, I went to college for three years to become a medical lab technician. Then I got a job at Cho Ray Hospital, where I received about 10,000 dong in Vietnamese money. I could buy nine kilos of rice, a half kilo of sugar, twenty grams of MSG, and sometimes even fish. It wasn't enough salary for one person, but compared with the rest of the people at the time, I was pretty lucky. Life was simple then, even though the government made many changes and watched my people so carefully.

I lived in a two-story house on Hung Phu Street, Ben Ba Dinh, near Y Bridge. I lived very comfortably in a middle-class family. After the North took over the South in April 1975, my parents moved back to Go Cong City near the ocean and resumed farming. During this period I had to take care of myself. I worked at Cho Ray Hospital for three years while many of my friends escaped the country because life became harsh. It was harder to survive under the new government, especially since the laws kept changing from day to day. I started to look for a way out also. It happened that my brother-in-law was an organizer for people to escape, and I made my first try with him, but it failed.

In my second attempt to escape, I boarded a small boat from Y Bridge in order to taxi to the main boat at Can Gio Island. On the island there were a lot of eucalyptus, cork tree, and dua nuoc groves; people use dua nuoc leaves to make thatch houses. Most of the residents who lived on this island were V.C. [Viet Cong] or their relatives or people who sympathized with the V.C. I boarded a boat two and half meters wide and ten meters long, which carried about 100 people. We departed at about 11:00 P.M. to Duyen Hai in order to get onto the ocean. But before we reached Duyen Hai, the police boat started chasing us. They shot at us and in the air to force the boat to stop. Our boat landed on the shore, and everyone ran in different directions. Chaos erupted. Shouting and cursing blended with dogs barking in the village. Under the dim moon, I ran toward houses with lights still on. I saw an open door and passed through it to the middle of the house.

"Where are you going? Stop it, stop it!" a woman yelled. I didn't pay any attention. I saw the bed and quickly crawled underneath, but two men were already there.

"Move over," I said. "Give me some room here." Then I pushed the person to the side and fit myself into the spot.

"Take it easy. I was here first," a male voice broke out.

I heard footsteps moving toward the bed. A woman in her fifties appeared with an oil lamp in her hands. She squatted down on the floor.

"You can't stay here, children," she said. "My son is a V.C. and the head of this village. He will be home soon. You can't hide anywhere on this island because they [the V.C.] will capture you anyway in the morning, since the island is isolated."

I crawled from under the bed. I knew now there was nowhere to hide. "Please help me. I don't want to spend time in jail," I begged the woman.

Then two men came from under the bed. They looked at the woman to see if what she said was true. The woman walked into the kitchen.

"The good thing is that no other V.C. will come to my house right now because they don't expect me to hide an escapee," she emphasized. "And I don't want to disappoint my son either. The only thing I can do for you right now is let you stay here for a while until the chase cools down. Then you will have to leave."

She placed an oil lamp on the wooden table and turned to the cabinet. She took a few dishes out and placed them in front of us.

"Sit down. Have something to eat because it will be a long night," she said.

I wondered if she was real or if she was just using a trick to capture us. She seemed honest and calm as if she had done this kind of thing before.

"I have some money here. Please help me," I asked again. "I will pay you."

She shook her head while she scooped rice into the bowls. "I couldn't do anything for you even if I wanted to."

The two men listened to see if the commotion outside had subsided, and after they heard the woman say that she couldn't help, they sneaked out of the house without saying anything. I sat down because I thought what was the point to escape if there was no way out. I picked up a bowl of rice and ate it. There were some steamed vegetables marinated with sesame oil, garlic, and soy sauce along with some fried catfish. I actually enjoyed the meal. I wasn't nervous or scared anymore. The woman was quiet and watched me eat. Then I heard voices getting closer to the house.

"Go, go," the woman said, getting up from the bench. "Go out the back door."

I ran out of the house, but I saw a few shadows approaching. I dove into a pile of hay next to the water buffalo and held my breath.

"Hello, Thiem Nam. Have you seen anyone pass through here? There was a boat of people who tried to escape earlier," a voice from the group called out to the woman inside the house. They stood near the buffalo.

"No, I haven't seen anybody," she yelled out. "I heard shooting at the river earlier—so that was the commotion. Where is my son, Hai?"

"He is at the river, Thiem Nam. He isn't done yet. He'll be home in a minute. Thank you, Thiem Nam. I'll tell him you are waiting for him. I'll see you in the morning," the voice answered.

They walked around the bushes, then passed by the pond where the coconut shadows swayed in the water, and disappeared in the moonlight. If they had had a dog, then I would have been in big trouble. I got out of the haystack and walked closer to the house. I stuck my head in the back door.

"Ma'am, please help me. I don't know what to do, and I know you have a good heart," I whispered to her.

"I thought you already left. What are you doing here?" she said. "Wait a minute."

She stood up from the bench and walked toward me. "There is a graveyard about five kilos from here." She pointed in the direction where the V.C. had gone. "There is a shack in the cemetery. Go there and hide, and I'll make some arrangements for you in the morning."

"Thank you, ma'am."

I ran to the trail and moved along a line of eucalyptus trees. There was a small river that followed the trail. I finally found a shack in the middle of the graveyard. I carefully approached it. It was quiet and empty. I found a spot in the corner where the caretaker of the graveyard stored his tools and materials. I lay down on the dirt and tried to sleep, but suddenly a chill hit my back. Then I realized this was a place for the dead. I was shaking. I was scared of ghosts because I used to hear stories about them when I was younger. I sat up and leaned against the wall. Mosquitoes were buzzing, and I heard a thump outside as if someone had thrown something at the door of the shack. Then I heard footsteps. I closed my eyes tightly and waited for something to happen. Nothing did. I opened my eyes and moved out of the shack, but my legs were heavy.

Where would I go if I didn't stay here, I asked myself. How would the woman find me in the morning? I thought I better stay put even though I would have to live with the dead for the night. I inched back to the same spot and grabbed a shovel and held it tightly. I wanted to go home. I wanted to see my parents. I didn't want to escape anymore. I kept repeating these thoughts in my head and then fell asleep.

As the woman promised, she came to the shack in the morning, with her nephew who was about my age, 19 years old. She woke me up, then instructed her nephew to row a boat to Ben Bach Dang for me. I paid her some money and thanked her for her help. She told me to change in order to look like a local girl because the V.C. had already set up checkpoints in every direction. I had to pretend to be her nephew's girlfriend. I had to learn how to paddle quickly so that I could sit in front of the boat and row while the boy rowed in the back. Her nephew sang a few lines of a song here and there whenever we approached a checkpoint, and since many of the V.C. knew him, they didn't stop him.

"Where are you going, Tinh?" a V.C. called out to us from the shore. "You better watch out for bandits. You never know what they are going to do if they want your boat."

"I am going to Bach Dang to buy a few things for Thiem Nam and take my girlfriend home," Tinh replied. "Thank you for the warning. I'll be careful."

I rowed and Tinh rowed, but I didn't see the boat move. Indeed, I just stirred the water like a kid playing. I pulled my conical hat lower, pretending the sun was in my eyes. We passed another checkpoint. The trip took two and a half hours. I was lucky not to be caught. I got off the boat and thanked Tinh. On my way home I was also lucky to meet the captain of the escape boat, the man who influenced the rest of my life. I went to a bus station and looked for a small bus to go back to my district because usually the police didn't check small buses. I got on and sat next to a man.

"It's hot today," I said, "and I am all messy. Farm work is hard." I tried to start a conversation to cover up my nervousness and the dirtiness of my clothes and my hair, but no one was in the mood to talk. The man sitting next to me just smiled as if he read me.

"Yes, farm work is hard," he said finally.

The driver called for the last boarding, started the engine, and then moved the bus out of the station. The dirt flew up, and passersby hurried to the side of the road to avoid the bus. The bus was crowded, and some people had to stand in the aisle or on the steps at the back. The bus traveled for 20 minutes without any incident, then finally pulled to a stop.

"Where do you live?" the man asked me. He held my hand to assist me off the bus.

"I live near Y Bridge."

"I know where it is. I live near there also," he said. "Maybe we can walk home together."

"My brother is supposed to pick me up, but if he doesn't show up, then I can walk home with you," I said, making it up. "He sent me to work at the farm."

"Why doesn't he work on the farm? He wants to ruin your beautiful hands," the man said, winking.

The man had a small frame. His eyes were alert and sharp. I liked them. There was something attractive about him, but I couldn't pinpoint it.

There were many people at the bus station and many police officers also. Because I was a bandit, I didn't want to cling to the man. If I was in trouble, then he would be involved, so I tried to get rid of him.

"My brother will be here in a minute," I said. "I hope to see you again."

He smiled at me and nodded his head.

"Sure, see you next time," he said as he walked away.

After a few minutes I realized that I didn't even ask him his name or where he lived or how the heck I would see him again. I smiled at myself. What a fool I was. I took a pedicab home. My sister was happy to see me. Nothing important was happening at home. And this time my sister advised me not to try to escape anymore, since I had missed two of my chances.

"At least let me try a third time, and if the third time I don't succeed, then I'll stay home for good," I told her.

I was no longer working for the hospital because of my absences. I opened a soda stand in front of my house, selling lemonade, sodas, Vietnamese Jell-O, and sam bo luong (an iced dessert). My older sister helped me set out a few tables and chairs and watched the stand for me while I ran for ice or got more supplies. Everything I bought was on the black market. Without the black market, the residents in Saigon would die. The irony was that the government declared it would get rid of the black market, but most of the people who worked for the government were the very ones who bought merchandise from the government and brought it here to sell on the black market. If the government wants to eliminate the underground market, they should get rid of poverty.

Before 1975 most people had jobs, and after 1975 nobody had a job except for the V.C. and Northerners. The government didn't use Southerners or anyone who was related to the former Southern government. Everyone was free now, free of having a job and free of thinking also because the government did the thinking for the people.

One of my regular customers was Hoa, a lady from Thu Thiem who sold tasty xoi bap treats. These are made of boiled corn mixed with shredded coconut meat and mung bean paste and a touch of sugar. She carried her two baskets with a yoke and walked all over the place to sell the treats. When she came to my stand, she was exhausted. I sold her my drinks, and she sold me her xoi. It became our daily routine. I learned more about her, and she got to know me better. She was small, with dark skin. Her eyes seemed to be baggy and sunk in her skull. She was 21. On her face, there was something missing—life, yes, life. She had one small boy, and the child's father was in a labor camp. She had to take care of her child, her parents, and a brother. She had to put meals on the table from the xoi treats that she sold. Along with the yoke, she carried many responsibilities and made many sacrifices. I didn't know if I could do it myself. My heart went out to her, but I couldn't do anything to help except to buy her xoi bap once a day. I knew a few dong from me didn't make any difference, but she could talk to me while she took a break from her work.

One day I went to my brother-in-law, Xang, to find out when he would dispatch the next group to escape so I could join them. I went to his house, and when I walked into the living room, I immediately saw the man I had met on the bus a few months earlier. My mouth dropped, and my heart bounced. I sat down on a chair, and my brother introduced me.

"This is Nho, our new captain for the next boat."

"Hello again," he said, smiling. "What a surprise! Is this your brother who sent you to work on the farm?"

I nodded my head. I couldn't say anything. I had totally forgotten him and now he was back.

"Do you know each other?" my brother-in-law asked.

"We met on the bus on my way home," he said calmly, like nothing had happened.

After that he came to my house to see me, and I went to my brother-in-law's to see him. We often talked about our future and our plans if we ever escaped from Vietnam. I learned more about his past. Nho was the first son, and his father had died when he was young. He had many brothers and sisters. Nho joined the navy after he graduated from high school because his family was poor and he couldn't afford to go to college. He also learned more about my family, how three of my brothers had worked for the South Vietnamese government. My family was against our relationship, but I didn't care. In September 1985 Nho and I got married. We had a simple wedding.

Two months after the wedding, we escaped. This time, with Nho as captain, we planned to depart from Vam Lang and travel through Go Cong, where my parents lived, to reach the sea. After collecting fuel and food and enough people to join in order to share the expenses, we bought a boat about eight meters long and two meters wide. This boat would transport about 80 people. We left Vam Lang around noon and reached Go Cong in the afternoon. We had to wait there in the river for nightfall before we could depart for the ocean. The boat was anchored at the side of the river covered by marsh bushes. Everyone hid under the deck, and the captain's crew laid low. Then suddenly I heard shooting coming from everywhere. People were panicking. They jumped out of the boat, some onto the land and others into the river. They ran in all directions. The police surrounded our boat.

"Stay where you are. We'll shoot if you move," a policeman shouted from the shore, as others aimed their guns at our boat. "Get on the deck and put your hands up."

The police patrol boat arrived, and they towed our boat to a nearby elementary school. The police escorted us to the school and ordered us to sit on the playground. There was barbed wire around the perimeter, and there was no place to hide or run. We spent the whole night at the school. Then the next day the police took us to the outskirts of My Tho and put us in a labor camp. They separated males and females, so I did not see my husband until two years later. My in-law, Xang, and his wife had tried to escape with us this time, and later Xang died in the camp. He didn't even know that his wife was pregnant. She hadn't told him because if she had, he wouldn't have planned to escape.

The camp looked like military barracks. There was a long roof held by pillars with no walls. Barbed wire surrounded the camp, and there was a river that ran alongside, where everyone bathed, did laundry, and washed dishes. There was only one gate. In front of it there was a pond where the guards raised ca tra, catfish. We built toilets above the pond for everyone to use. The catfish would digest our human waste. It was the same kind of open-sewage system that most Third World countries use.

We slept on a dirt floor in a spot designated for us by the guard. Each spot was the size of a twin bed. There were 150 prisoners there. If you were there for a long time, you could collect some throwaway wood and build yourself a pallet. You would sleep on it at night, and you would put it away in the morning like your own bed. If you had slept on the dirt floor, then you would appreciate sleeping on the pallet. At night the ground was cold, and people could get sick easily.

Every prisoner received two meals a day. Each meal contained one bowl of rice and a teaspoon of salt. Whenever there was a big holiday, like on April 30, an inmate would get an extra bowl of vegetables, rau muong soup, and one piece of salty pork the size of my thumb. (April 30 was a day of celebration for the Communists and a day of sadness for the South because it was the day Saigon had fallen.)

I sent home the bad news of my capture to my sister, through the visiting relative of another inmate. I listed what I needed so that my sister could bring these things to me. The list included a plastic bucket to use for laundry and to scoop water up from the river. I also asked for toothpaste, a toothbrush, a bowl, and a pair of chopsticks. One smaller bucket I could use for my bedpan at night because the guard let the inmates get only a 30-minute break a day to bathe, use the toilet, do laundry, or whatever. In exchange for these privileges, the prisoner had to labor from 5:00 in the morning until 6:00 in the evening. I had to learn how to make straw mats, hats, and baskets. I liked it. It was tedious work, but it killed the time. Besides, I learned a new skill. The guards divided us into groups, and we had to produce a certain quota a day. The guards took these products and sold them at the market. I hated the part when the guard lectured us about how wonderful it was to labor and how wonderful Ho Chi Minh and the Communist Party were. When he ended his lecture, we always had to write our confession.

If a prisoner pooped at night in her bucket and stunk the whole place, then we cursed her.

"What did you eat today? Did you eat shit?" we shouted. "Stop pooping. It stinks. If you poop like this once more, then we will throw you into the catfish pond and let the catfish eat you alive."

"Who is pooping? Check your perimeter," a guard's loud voice would break out.

"She is right here," someone in the corner would reply.

"Tell the guard in the morning and ask him to sign her up for a longer reform," the same loud voice would say.

"She deserves it. She doesn't understand our policy yet. She doesn't thoroughly understand Uncle Ho and our Party. She needs to study and labor harder."

We went on for half an hour until we were tired of talking or until they yelled at us to shut up. I felt kind of funny because people never really showed exactly who they were until they were in the bottom of life like in this case. I was in a predicament, but I was learning, and there was no school that could teach me all this better than the school of life.

My sister came to visit me and brought the materials on the list. I asked her to visit my husband also and to let me know how he was doing. My sister bribed the guard and made arrangements for me to get out earlier, and after eight months in the camp I got out. I went back home, and my parents begged me not to try to escape again because it was too dangerous. I told them not to worry. I had run out of money and resources, but wondered what I could do if I stayed. I thought especially of my husband. The government had never accepted him as a citizen. We would never have a normal family under the new government. The more I thought about it, the more I wanted to flee.

I knew my brother had a connection with a cashew company owned mostly by the government, so I asked him to get me in. I got a job as a manager of 150 people, and I made ten times the salary I had made at the hospital. While I worked at this company, I made plans for me and my husband. I used the money to bribe the guards at my husband's camp to get him out. I visited him once every month, and after spending two years in the camp, Nho got out, in July 1987.

In September 1987, he and I boarded a boat at Ham Luong. Again my husband was the captain. We aimed for Ben Tre and reached the sea without any incident. I spent three nights and four days with 73 people on a rickety boat sailing directly to Pulau Bidong. We landed at this refugee camp and joined 20,000 refugees already there. We got our immunization shots and received food supplies once a week: salt, fish sauce, and canned sardines. We lived with three other families and shared a small cabin four meters by six with a loft above. It was too crowded, and life was harsh. The authorities here didn't allow refugees to fish or net, but sometimes I could buy fish on the underground market. If the authorities caught you, they would punish you.

I volunteered to work for the clinic in the camp. The clinic had ten beds and one foreign doctor. When I had more time, I learned how to type, and some friends taught me some English. There were beaches where I could swim, and there was a public television where I could watch a movie or the news.

After the people from the U.N. High Commissioner for Refugees interviewed us, the American consulate interviewed and accepted us. It had been four months since we came to the camp. Our acceptance was very fast compared with that of many other refugees who had been there before us. I was happy and excited that we would be settling in America. I didn't have to worry anymore. My husband and I just waited.

In February 1988 the authorities moved us to Sungei Besi, Malaysia. We stayed there for two months, with 5,000 other refugees. This camp was much better than Pulau Bidong. Sungei Besi was situated on a hill, but I could not see any ocean around. We received instant noodles for breakfast and got three full meals a day. The camp had a public bathroom, and every family had its own quarters to live in. We signed up for English class.

In April 1988 once again we moved, this time to Bataan in the Philippines. There were Vietnamese, Cambodians, and Laotians in the camp. It was better furnished than other camps because any refugee who came to this camp already had been accepted by the United States. We had to study about United States culture and the English language for six months before we could leave. The authorities had a schedule for us to follow. I received rice and other food supplies once every two days and always had more than I had had in the other camps. I could take a shower at the quarters where I stayed. I felt like I was moving up in the world. There was a waterfall where everyone could go swimming. Bataan was the most memorable place for me because it was the place I told my husband that I was pregnant with our first child. That happiness came at the same time that we heard our names called to go to Manila for our departure to the United States.

In September 1988 we flew from Manila to San Francisco, where we stayed overnight. The next day we continued to our final destination: Manchester, New Hampshire. Our sponsor, Ann, who worked for a nonprofit agency, came to the airport to greet us and took us by van to an apartment on Pennacook Street. We settled in our new place. It was a shabby apartment, but for us it meant more because we had each other and we were safe from our war-torn country. My country would be forever in my heart whether I ever had a chance to return.

In the next few days, my husband and I had medical checkups, applied for Social Security cards, registered with the employment department, and tried to find out about any English class in the community. Ann took care of the welfare application so that we could get some money to pay the rent and get food stamps. Before long my husband got a job at Felton Brush, making all kinds of brushes including brushes for industries. I worked for Pandora Company, making clothing. We made the minimum wage, $4.25 an hour. At Pandora I worked for a few days, then they laid me off. Then they called me back when they had orders. It wasn't stable, and I didn't like it because I felt that I had been used. Since they needed me to work for only a few days, when they ran out of things to do they sent me home. I was a call girl. I felt cheap and cheated. I was disappointed because I worked very hard. I learned the first lesson in America: no company wanted to care for their workers. It was just a job. It wasn't like that in Vietnam before 1975. The workers worked wholeheartedly for the company, and the company cared for them.

My belly started to show, and it was harder for me to look for another job, so I stuck with Pandora for more than a year, until I gave birth to Sarah in May 1989. After that I started to look for something different and came to the refugee community center, which opened in December 1989 across the street from my apartment. I talked to Olga, the employment specialist, who explained the opportunities I had and helped me to land a better job. I found a job at a cable company. It wasn't so good either, but I learned a new skill and it was lighter work than at Pandora. I worked at Carrol Cable for three years. I was still looking for a better-paying job with a better environment. Then a friend of mine helped me get a job at an electronics company as a board tester. I worked for a year, then got laid off again. I wanted to go to school, but since I had to make a living and take care of my child and the apartment, I didn't have much time to spare for any classes. This period was the most unproductive, and I changed jobs more than in my whole life in Vietnam. Finally, I found an electronics tester position at Micro Tech through a temporary agency, and later the job became permanent. I had to commute back and forth to Nashua for work, but I thought it was worth it because I made $7 dollar an hour. I'm still working there. My husband and I bought a house in 1992, and we moved into a new neighborhood. It was quiet, and Sarah had a good school to go to.

When I arrived in the United States I had a hard time adjusting to the new environment, especially the language. I liked living in Vietnam better than America. There I always had my family support and a close relationship with my brothers, sisters, and other relatives. In America I don't have this kind of support. Life in America is too stressful and isolated, although material goods are always plentiful. I wish I could return to live in Vietnam when I get old. I want to live near my family back home.

One of the things I don't like is that children in the United States seem never to want to listen to their parents. It's not like in Vietnam.

I like to work, and actually I'm a workaholic. But I don't like my job because it's not suitable for me. I was trained as a lab technician, but I have to work as an electronics tester at a factory, and on the weekend I work at a restaurant. I want to get back into the lab technician field, but I would have to go to school again. Besides, I wouldn't have much time to spend with my children. In Vietnam you had a lot of time to spend with your children, but you had to work really hard there. You worked hard, but you still didn't have enough to live on. Living in Vietnam is living in fear and uncertainty. I would never know what would happen the next day.

In May 1993 I took my daughter, Sarah, then four years old, to Vietnam to visit her grandparents. I packed her clothes and mine in one bag. I took the nicest dresses I had and my makeup kit. I was anxious to go, but at the same time I felt things might have changed so much in Vietnam that I wouldn't recognize them. I wondered what the place would look like and if my relatives would recognize me. It had been seven years.

I said goodbye to my husband and left Boston. We stopped over in Seoul, then flew directly to Thanh Pho Ho Chi Minh. I arrived the evening of the next day, on May 27. When the captain announced that we were approaching Tan Son Nhut International Airport, I glued my eyes to the window. Below there were thousands of lights glowing from yellow to red to blue. Saigon seemed to be alive. I didn't know what was waiting for me down there. My heart pounded heavily. The aircraft descended closer to the bright lights and landed safely.

"Welcome to TP Ho Chi Minh City. This is your captain speaking. The local time is 10:25 p.m., and the temperature outside right now is 97 degrees. On behalf of our crew, I'd like to thank you for choosing Korean Airlines. We were glad to serve you, and we look forward to serving you again. I hope you have a pleasant time in Saigon or whatever your destination may be."

Are you sure I will have a pleasant stay? I thought. The aircraft came to a complete stop. I stood up and gathered my belongings and woke Sarah, then followed the passengers to the gate. When I went through immigration and customs, I had to place $5 or $10 bills in my papers at every checkpoint since other Vietnamese passengers had warned me on the airplane: "Bribe them. Otherwise they give you a lot of hassle or trouble." It was hot and humid, and I perspired. I wondered if the weather or nervousness made me sweat.

Sarah and I got out of the customs office, and I saw my brother and his wife and children waiting for us. They hugged me and Sarah. We cried. We went home in my brother's van. I asked about my parents and other sisters and brothers.

"Men is still in jail. The authorities will release him when it's quiet outside, but if there is something happening around town, then they will take him back to jail," my brother Diep said. I was exhausted, but I liked to watch the scenery that I hadn't seen for seven years. Half an hour later we were in the center of town. There were so many bicycles, motorbikes, cars, and pedicabs. It was congested and dirty. Around Nguyen Hue Circle there were stands and stands of flowers for sale. Street lights shone like at Christmas. I wondered who would buy these flowers when there was so much poverty. I bet in any society there is only one group that always has that privilege—the higher officer and the one who has money. We passed by Ben Bach Dang Wharf, where there was a floating Australian restaurant, Uc Dai Loi. It was a five-star restaurant and the most expensive place to eat. It was packed and lively like a festival. I saw many tourists among the locals. The lights, the noises, the crowd, the water, the air, the aroma of food and the open sewage mixed together to make me drowsy. My brother drove a few times around the block, then we headed home.

We arrived home at 8:00 P.M. My parents, sister, brother, and relatives came out to greet me. I grabbed my mother and hugged her, then my father. We all cried. Their hair had already turned shades of salt and pepper. When I had left home, their hair was still black and my parents looked vibrant, but now they were thinner and their faces were all wrinkled like ocean ripples. I felt a warmness, and I kissed them again and again. Then I held everyone and we whispered a few lines of greeting, but actually no one was listening. There was no language. We said it all in our hearts. My mother took Sarah in her arms.

"So this is my grandchild!" she said, touching her hair. "You look just like your mother, but I hope you don't have her stubborn head." She put Sarah down on the cement floor and held her hand.

"Come, come inside. It's getting late." My mother invited everyone in.

My father asked me about our trip and about my husband. We had a late dinner, and we talked to catch up with things since the time I had left. Not much had changed, I said to myself. My soda stand was gone, and the front court was empty. The plum tree in the corner was still green, and the vines were crawling higher on the cement fences. I felt smaller. The house seemed old, perhaps because it hadn't been painted. My ancestors' altar stood erect, and the burning incense fragrance was in the air. I used to light incense every morning and evening for my ancestors. This was my ritual. On the wall a few plaques were hanging, telling folk tales.

I remembered these stories well when I was in school. The house became noisier, and people were in and out as they are during the holidays. I went to bed late that night and didn't get up until 11:00 the next morning.

I rested at home for a few days to recuperate from my long trip. Sarah was happy, but she asked about her father. I told her we would return to see him soon. One Saturday afternoon I put on my best dress and put some makeup on and asked Diep to take me around town. I went to Cho Lon, the famous Chinatown in the suburbs of Saigon. It had grown bigger. There were more businesses and malls than in Cho Ben Thanh, the center of Saigon. The merchandise at Cho Lon also was cheaper. I bought a few new blouses and looked for a small Chinese dress for Sarah, but nothing fit her. She was too skinny. We left Cho Lon and headed for So Thu and Vuon Tao Dan Zoo and Garden so that Sarah could enjoy herself.

I bought tickets and we entered. This place used to be beautiful, and every Saigon resident could come to take a stroll under the shade of trees or to watch exotic animals, but now it was ruined. It was dirty, and litter was everywhere. Trees and flowers seemed to be tattered, as if no one was taking care of them. Most of the animals were gone, and the remaining ones depressed me because they looked sick, and they were so thin. I wondered if they were ever fed. They were not only living in cages, but they were starving. I knew for sure now why I had escaped from my country. I didn't want to suffer or to die the way these animals had. The heat began to aggravate me, and I didn't want Sarah to see the scene any longer. I didn't have any language to explain it to her. We went home.

The next day I visited my husband's family in Ba Ria District. He had nine brothers and sisters. They were farmers, and this year they had lost their crops because of the drought. The durian, mang cau dai, and jackfruit trees didn't produce. Life was tough for his brothers and sisters. They had children to feed and a mother to take care of, and I could not help. I dressed in nice clothes and wore makeup. I didn't last a whole day at my husband's home before I hurried back to Saigon. I gave away my makeup, new blouses, and best dresses. I went to the local market and bought local clothes to wear, although my conscience didn't leave me alone. I also gave most of my money to relatives. I kept just enough for my spending until the day I departed. I was one of the locals now, but people still recognized me because my skin seemed whiter and sometimes Sarah had to say something in English. I had no place to go now, so I stayed inside most of the time. I couldn't wait to go back to my husband. Sometimes my distant relatives stopped by to visit me, but I tried to avoid them because I didn't want to know their situation. I had nothing to offer them, nothing to comfort them. I hoped they understood my situation also. I wasn't rich in America. I was a coolie just like anybody else. I wasn't a successful Vietnamese businessperson. How many successful Vietnamese are there in America?

Perhaps I returned not only because I wanted to see my parents for the last time, but also because in Vietnam, people could make me feel like I was somebody. They treated me like a foreigner who had money. Didn't everybody want to be somebody? I didn't have an education or any skills, but I had the hope that my children would do better than me. I was a boat person, a refugee, and I was still on the boat. Sometimes I wondered where I would be anchored.

There was a boy about seven years old who wandered on the street to sell treats, *banh tieu* and *banh cong*, to make ends meet for his family. He was supposed to be in school, but instead of learning in school, he learned on the street. Every morning he carried the treats basket and walked along the sidewalk in front of my house. He called out, "*Banh tieu, banh cong*. It's warm when you take a bite. Buy some."

I took Sarah to the gate and called him. I bought the whole basket for only two American dollars. I fed Sarah, and she liked it. I brought them in for the whole family to eat, and I kept doing it every morning until nobody could eat *banh tieu* and *banh cong* anymore. I didn't ask his name. I didn't talk. I just wanted to buy his treats.

"Do you have *banh tieu* and *banh cong* in America?" my mother asked me.

"Yes, Mother, but they're more tasty at home," I replied.

My mother smiled at me, her face all wrinkled up as if she were ready to cry.

The next day I was playing with Sarah in front of the courtyard, waiting for the boy. But he never showed up. I didn't know what had happened to him. "Come boy, come. I'll buy your treats even if no one wants to eat them. I can give them away," I mumbled.

"Fresh *xoi bap*, fresh *xoi bap*," a woman called out on the street instead of the boy. The voice was very familiar, and I tried to remember where I had heard it, but I couldn't. I went to the gate. "*Xoi bap, xoi bap*," I called after the woman.

The woman walked in my direction, and her flip-flops made a "shiss shoos" sound. On her shoulder was a yoke, and it seemed heavy for her. Two baskets on both sides of the yoke were almost touching the ground. She swayed back and forth like an old train trying to move. From the distance I couldn't see her face clearly, since she wore a conical hat, called a *non la*. She came to the front gate and placed the two baskets on the pavement, then lay the yoke on the ground. She was dressed in a brown blouse, *ao ba ba*, and black fabric pants. She pulled out a small piece of wood like a tiny stand from the side of the basket, set it down in the middle of the two baskets, then sat on it. She took a breath, tilted her *non la*, and looked up at me.

"Can I..."

She didn't complete the sentence. I stared at her. Her mouth dropped wider. I shook my head.

"Hoa!" I exclaimed.

She stood up and reached for me. "Nhan!"

Her body shivered, and I felt like I was embracing a skeleton. It had been only seven years since I had seen her, and she had changed this much, I thought. She was in her thirties, but she looked like an old woman. I almost didn't recognize her. She had lost her front teeth, and her lips sunk into her gums.

"Where have you been? I thought you had moved," she said, releasing me. "I have been passing through your streets every day, and I never saw you after you closed the soda stand. I was afraid to come in and ask. You know the situation nowadays."

"Yes, I had moved. I got married," I answered. "I just came back to visit my relatives."

I didn't want to tell her where I lived, since I didn't want her to feel bad. If she knew that I lived in America, she may have had the wrong impression, like everybody else.

"You look younger," she said. "Do you have any kids? Is your husband here with you?"

She squeezed my hands and studied me.

"I look the same because I don't have to do a lot of hard work. My husband takes good care of me," I replied. "He didn't come this time, but I have my baby with me."

I called Sarah by her nickname in Vietnamese and introduced her to Hoa. Hoa extended her hands to Sarah, but Sarah withdrew.

"She's shy," I said. "You have to spend a few hours with her before she will talk to you."

"She's cute and healthy," Hoa complimented Sarah.

Hoa sat down and opened her baskets. She took a piece of banana leaf in her hand and scooped some boiled corn on the leaf, then placed the shredded coconut meat and mung bean paste, and sprinkled some sugar on the top. She wrapped it and handed it to Sarah. Sarah grabbed it and ran into the house.

"I wish you could meet my boy. He's eight now and he helps me out everyday by selling *banh tieu* and *banh cong* on this same route."

Hoa paused for a breath. "He's sick today. I had another child since his father came back from the labor camp. But his father died because of a wound from torture in the camp. Life has been a struggle for my eight year old from the start, but I am very proud of him." Her eyes sparkled. "He sells the treats very well and lately he's doing much better. When he isn't selling treats, he plays and keeps his sister busy."

Was Hoa perhaps talking about the boy I bought the treats from? I thought.

"That is wonderful, Hoa. Maybe I can meet him someday," I said. "I am sorry about your husband."

Hoa looked down at the ground and made a few more *xoi bap* wraps. She handed them to me. I saw her eyes were wet and her chest was heaving. There was no sound. I pulled out some dong to pay for the treats. Hoa refused to take the money.

"If you don't take my money, I am not going to eat your *xoi bap* next time," I said. "I don't feel right."

I knew damn well that there wouldn't be a next time. After I went back to the United States, how long would it take me to return to Vietnam again? Maybe I wouldn't return for a long time, and maybe, for many reasons, I wouldn't come back at all.

Finally Hoa took the money. She put everything away, then picked up the yoke and stuck it into a wire hook for the two baskets.

"I have to go and sell the rest of the *xoi bap*. It's nice to see you, Nhan," Hoa said, smiling at me. "If you're still around, I will see you again."

Hoa put her *non la* on, bent down slightly, placing her shoulder in the middle of the yoke, and lifted the baskets.

"Say hello to your boy for me, and I hope he'll get well soon," I said and forced a grin.

Hoa walked slowly down the street. I stood at the gate, watching her until she disappeared at the end of the corner.

"Fresh *xoi bap*, fresh *xoi bap*," I heard Hoa's voice echo from the distance.

I brought the *xoi bap* into the house and placed them on a wooden table in the kitchen. I saw my mother playing with Sarah. I came and hugged both of them. What if Sarah were in the boy's shoes? What if I were in Hoa's circumstances? My mother started to prepare the afternoon meal. I went upstairs to my room and lay down. The sun shone through the window where I used to stand when I returned home from school on a stormy day. I watched the doves on top of the opposite building in a hurry to look for a place to hide and wondered where I would fly if I knew how. I reached for an old electric fan and turned it on. The fan stirred the humid air, and it made a purring sound like a cat. I fell asleep.

The last day before I went back to America I wanted to make dinner for my family, so I got up early, around 7:00 A.M. I asked my mother to watch Sarah for me, then I dressed up. I took a straw bag and walked to the dock to catch a ferry from Y Bridge to District Five to go to the market. Actually, this ferry was like the boat I escaped on. It carried only passengers and bicycles. It was a shortcut to Saigon downtown and Cho Ben Thanh.

The market was crowded and dirty. It was like a flea market in America. People displayed their merchandise on a stand, and we picked what we wanted and bargained for it. I bought *ca ro* and yellow catfish, ginger, green onion, Chinese cabbage, and a half kilo of boneless pork. I also got some oranges, one papaya, *oi* (guava), and *man* (plum) to offer to my ancestors.

After I made sure I had everything, I went back to the ferry and got on. I paid for my fare and sat on a bench. The ferry was waiting for more passengers. The tide was low now, and the mud on both sides of the river looked black like an oil spill. People had built houses on the mud supported by tree trunks. The walls were wrapped around with billboards or pieces of metal. The roofs, made of leaves or plastic, were held down by bamboo strips or ropes. I hardly saw any black tires on the roofs, since people had used them all. They used the tires to make sandals and for household use. I had seen a lot of tires on roofs before 1975, but not now. Indeed these houses were shacks, and the place was a slum. Garbage was everywhere: papers, broken cups, plastic bags, empty cans, cigarette butts, human waste, and anything one could find at a dump. A curtain of gas bubbled and evaporated. I breathed the stench of gas and felt as if I were buried inside a sewage pipe. The water was brown and black like Coca-Cola.

I noticed a group of children, all the size of the boy who sold treats to me, scampering in the mud and beneath the houses. Each one of them held a stick. They poked at a plastic bag or reached for a rubber band floating on the water or for anything they could sell for recycling. A thin boy stood near the ferry dock. He looked like he had only bones and skin without any flesh. His eyes were bulging, and his skin was dark, probably because he wore no shirt. He wore shorts, but they had holes and patches like a quilt. He poked at a nylon bag, then unhooked it. He tucked the bag into his shorts, and the water dripped down his leg. The engine of the ferry was revving, and it seemed to bother him. He tilted his head and looked at the ferry, then went back to his activities. He put his stick in his other hand and reached for his head. He scratched it, then rubbed his nose, leaving mud stains on his face. The ferry headed across the river. I went home, but I couldn't forget the boy's face. I couldn't forget the scene at the dock. What could I do? How could I help them? I wondered if what Confucius said was true, "Helping yourself is helping others."

In the afternoon, I roasted *ca ro* and yellow catfish, and I made ginger fish sauce for the dish. Then I ground the boneless pork and marinated it with fish sauce, a touch of sugar, a bit of green onion, and black pepper. I rolled it into a small ball and wrapped it with the cabbage to make cabbage soup.

All of my family members joined me for dinner and said an early goodbye to me. I tried to laugh with them, but my heart was lost. My heart was not the only thing that was lost. I also lost myself somewhere between Vietnam and America.

I went back to America the next day. My husband was happy to see me and Sarah. He asked me so many questions about home in Vietnam, but I didn't know how to explain it to him. I couldn't answer his questions. I returned to work. I thought about everything I had done, but I could not find an answer for myself either. I thought perhaps I should not ask anything at all because the more I asked, the more questions arrived. Five months after my return to the United States, my father had to answer his own question, and he answered it without asking any more. He passed away. I wanted to go home to take him back to Go Cong for his final resting place, but I couldn't afford it. I miss you, Baba, and I wish you could share your wonderful life with us again. And in January 1995, I received an answer. I gave birth to a baby boy, and I asked myself, where is my boy coming from and where is he going? Home, I guess. But is it really his or is it really mine? Where is home?

Chapter 16

To the Land of Snow

Hien Trong Nguyen escaped from Vietnam by boat on July 7, 1984. He attended high school in Manchester, New Hampshire, and later made a home there with his wife, Linda, whom he married in 1997. As of this writing Hien worked at Kollsman Inc. in Merrimack and was studying toward his associate's degree. Stephen Berwick has known Hien since 1989 and is proud to be his friend and to be considered his *anh trai*, his elder brother.

I was born in Saigon on December 12, 1969. My father, Nguyen Van Ty, and my mother, Bui Thi Yeu, both Catholics, had immigrated to South Vietnam in 1954, not long after the Communist takeover of the North. My parents moved at a time when there was a mass exodus of people fleeing the poverty and political situation in the North. The South, especially Saigon, was like a beacon to the impoverished Northerners. In the South the economy was strong, entrepreneurship was common, and people could make a good living, with a chance to enjoy life.

I was the youngest of three brothers and four sisters. My oldest brother, Nguyen Trong Nham, who was a second lieutenant (*thieu uy*) in the Southern army, was killed during the Vietnam War. I still carry the bloodstained photograph of him that he had in his shirt pocket the day he was shot. I will never forget him. My oldest brother and I were very close. He could always make me laugh. Whenever he came home on furlough, he would take me to a movie theater, carrying me on his shoulders so that I could see the movie better. When he died in 1974, he was only 22 years old. Five years after my brother's death, the Communists plowed the cemetery for Southern soldiers, where my brother was buried, in order to build a military training center. My mother decided to exhume his body and move him. During the next few days, my parents, uncle, cousins, and I went to remove his body. When I first looked at his body, I was amazed and frightened to see that he looked as if he were only sleeping. His body was wrapped inside a plastic bag, and the coffin had been specially made so that water would not seep in. My family took his body and removed all the skin and flesh so that only bones remained. The skin came off just like a glove. The bones were washed and put in a smaller box. My brother's body was moved to another cemetery, where we fit the box into a wall along with boxes containing other bodies. His name was attached to the front of the wall, along with his photograph.

A year later the Communists decided to change this place into a playground. We had to move his body once again. This time my parents decided to cremate him. My brother's ashes were placed in an urn, and he now finally rests in a church. Even after all the years that had gone by, my mother still couldn't get over the fact that her son had died. Every time we had to move his body, it was like watching him die all over again. My mother couldn't understand why the Communists couldn't just leave him alone. After all, he was dead—he was no threat to the Communists now. My mother suffered so much pain because of this. This was her eldest son, the one in whom so many dreams had rested.

Before the fall of Saigon, my father worked as a security guard at a movie studio while my mother stayed home and took care of the house and children. After the war, my father retired and stayed home, where he sold rice and gas from a stall in front of our house. My family was middle class—not wealthy, not poor—and our house on Xo Viet Nghe Tinh Road was like any other house in Saigon.

I don't remember much about the war years because I was too young. However, after the Communist takeover, life became very difficult for all Southerners, especially for those families with ties to the old government, no matter how loose those ties were. Since my oldest brother had worked for the South, we had difficulties. For example, my brothers and sisters had all finished high school, but they could not go to college. Only those people who were Communist Party members could go to college.

When I was about 15 years old, I began peddling cigarettes, selling them to all the restaurants near my house; at night I would sell them in bars and cafes. Sometimes people would challenge me by giving me a glass of beer and telling me that if I could drink it in one gulp, they would buy a pack of cigarettes from me. I guess that's when I learned how to drink and smoke cigarettes. I also started working with my brother-in-law, helping him to rebuild trucks.

Our life went along without much incident until Vietnam started sending troops into Cambodia to fight against the Khmer Rouge, who had invaded the border areas with Vietnam. Because my elder brother had died in the war, my parents didn't want to see another son die that way. It was because of this that my parents had to make a very difficult decision. They had heard of ways to escape the country, so they checked around and found out all the details. They decided my third brother and I must escape or we would be killed in the fields of Cambodia. My third brother left Vietnam in 1982 and now lives in Canada. I left two years later.

I left my family during the daytime. It was the most difficult and painful decision I have ever had to make. I couldn't bear to leave my family, my friends, everything I knew. My parents had no idea where I would end up, but they trusted that God would take care of me. Even though my parents knew that many people had died trying to escape the country, they felt the risk was worth it.

It cost my family $2,000 in gold to get me a place on the boat. The first night after I left my house, I stayed with another family. Then, on the night of July 7, 1984, I began the escape from my homeland. I left with 74 other people aboard a fishing boat 12 meters long by 2½ meters wide from the village of Can Tho, located south of Saigon on the Mekong River.

An hour after we set out along the Mekong, heading toward the ocean, Communist patrol boats spotted us. They gave us a warning by flashing lights at our boat. But our captain turned the engine all the way up and tried to outrun them. Fifteen minutes later our boat was shot at. During this time the container holding our water supply was hit, and we lost all our water. One man was killed when a bullet hit him. He was a friend of mine who had worked with me in arranging the people and their belongings on the boat. The soldiers kept shooting until they ran out of small bullets. Then they began shooting M-79s. The soldiers shot three M-79s but couldn't hit the boat, though they came close. If one of the shots had hit us, our boat would have been blown into small pieces. Luckily, our boat was not hit this time. For over an hour the patrol boats chased us along the Mekong until we finally outran them. However, the engine had become so hot that it started to burn up; we had to turn it off. We were so close to the ocean that the strong tide kept pushing us backward down the river. At one point we struck a huge pole sticking up out of the water. Fishermen use poles like these to hook up nets to catch fish. We were stuck there for over an hour and were afraid our boat would be damaged. Fishing boats came toward us to get their catch, but when they saw us they were afraid we would rob them of their boats, so they went back to their village. We were afraid they would report us to the police and we would be arrested and thrown into prison for trying to escape. Everyone prayed for God's help. Eventually, with all the men struggling to push the boat away from the pole, we were able to break away.

It was morning by the time we left the Mekong behind and entered the South China Sea. Our engine began running again, and we were able to go forward without a problem. On this first morning out on the ocean we saw a Soviet ship. We didn't want to get close to it because we were afraid the Soviets would tow us back to Vietnam. Our boat's engine ran for one more day and night, but by the next morning the battery was dead. The engine was so big that we needed a battery to start it. Since the battery was gone, we couldn't do anything with the engine. We had nothing to make a sail with, so we couldn't capture the wind. From this time on we began to worry about our food supply. Because of the waves, the rice had become wet and salty so we couldn't use it. We had to ration the rice that was left—10 to 20 grains of rice per person a day, along with only a few drops of water. It was just enough to survive on. We had only enough water to survive for two days, and we didn't know what we could do to obtain water. When the rain came, it lasted only a short time, so we couldn't capture any water. We decided to use engine oil to burn clothes so that we could capture the steam as it escaped from the condensation of boiling seawater.

On the 17th day at sea, the woman who sat next to me began passing out from lack of food and water. The next morning she was dead. When I saw her dead body, I began to worry that in a few days I would become just like her. From that point on, I began believing that my life was in the hands of God. During the next two days, two more people died from hunger. From then on, every morning one or two people died. Most of the people who died were men ages 18 to 25. We men were weakened because we gave our rations to the women and children. We also lost a lot of energy from the effort of using containers to bail water out of the boat. I volunteered once to give out the rations, but from the 20th day on I became so weak that I couldn't do this work anymore.

Whenever we saw a ship, we would throw a corpse overboard to show we needed help. None of us had been able to take a shower for 30 days, so our boat really stank. Our boat smelled of oil, sweat, open scabs, excrement, and death.

Even though we saw many ships, none of them paid attention to us. When I saw this, I became extremely discouraged, began to hate other countries, and began to lose hope for life.

We had been stuck on the boat for 30 days when a Filipino fisherman spotted our boat and pulled us to the island of Batangas. From our boat, 17 people had died and 57 people were left. We had originally left Vietnam with enough provisions for three days. After we were rescued, we were taken to a camp hospital. I don't know how long I was in the hospital because I was unconscious. I only know that when I awoke, a new life had begun for me. I had beaten death.

We stayed in Batangas until the U.N. people began interviewing and photographing us. I was in the camp for seven days before we were all moved to a temporary place in Manila. We stayed there for two weeks so that we could recover, and were given special foods to enable us to get our energy back.

From Manila we went to Palawan Refugee Camp, still in the Philippines. I stayed at Palawan for one and a half years without any relatives or friends. It was so difficult, and I felt so lonely. We were able to move about the camp freely, but if we left the camp, we had to come back by a certain time.

I studied English and read books about life in America. After one and a half months of living in the camp, the United States government accepted me for resettlement in America under the Unaccompanied Minors Program. On November 18, 1985, I left the Philippines. I flew from Manila to Tokyo and then to San Francisco. While in Japan I had wanted to see my brother who was in a camp there, but because I had no money, I couldn't go see him. I felt so sad about that. I stayed in San Francisco for two weeks while my papers were processed, before going on to my foster family in New Hampshire. Life was difficult for the first six months while I tried to adapt. First of all, the landscape was so different. I was accustomed to the tropics, and now I was in a land covered with snow. I was really amazed and happy when I saw snow for the first time, but because it was so different, I began feeling regret for having left Vietnam and my family. Before coming to America I didn't have these feelings, but once the reality hit me that I was now in my new life, the sadness and solitude came. I had also arrived just before Christmas, which made it all the more difficult being away from my homeland. My first Christmas away from home had been in the Philippines, where the landscape is not too different from that of Vietnam.

It was also hard to adapt to life with an American family. There were many misunderstandings. Because I couldn't speak English well, I couldn't express myself or my feelings. Sometimes little problems arose, and my foster parents became angry with me for something I did, or something they thought I had done, and I had to try to explain my point of view to them. I would get angry and frustrated at myself because I could not make my foster parents understand me.

In addition to the language, the food and customs were difficult to adjust to. My parents in Vietnam had expected so much of me, and now at the same time my new parents expected much of me. Sometimes I felt that life wasn't worth living and that no one understood my heart.

After the first six months, I had to move to another foster family because of the difficulties with my first foster parents. I started high school as a freshman in November 1985. From my sophomore year on, I began to work and study so that I could become self-sufficient. My foster parents also taught me how to be independent. After graduation from high school, I began paying rent to them. The summer after graduation, I moved into the dormitory at New Hampshire Technical Institute, where I am now pursuing a degree in electronics engineering. Although I've had to stop my studies in order to make money, I plan to finish my degree so that I can become a technician at Kollsman.

When I returned to Vietnam in 1994, I felt so happy to be home again. Although the country had improved in many ways, the poor were still poor and the rich were still rich. I hope that some day my homeland will become better and that everyone will have enough to live. My father died in September 1997, at 72. I felt so bad because I was unable to go back. I had just gotten married in July, and there were a lot of expenses that I had to take care of. I wanted to go back to say goodbye to my father so much. It was a big sorrow for me. My dad waited for my brother and me to return. We called and told him that we couldn't make it. He then closed his eyes and left the world. My heart left with him.

When it rains I become sad and lonely and miss my country. Christmas and Tet, the Vietnamese New Year, are also difficult times for me. During these holidays I was always with my family—celebrating, sharing, and enjoying each other's company. My family is Roman Catholic, and I can't forget the way we celebrated Christmas in Vietnam. During the morning of December 24, we would decorate our house with a manger. During the evening we would go to Mass at the church and then go home and celebrate with family and friends and special foods. Tet was a time when the whole country celebrated. The house was decorated with branches of miniature yellow plum blossoms (*mai*) and mandarin orange trees. We ate special foods like sweet rice cooked with coconut, and we children received little red packets filled with money from our elders.

I can't forget my past or my family. It bothers me that I'm not able to help my family who still have to live under the Communist government. I suppose this is what I regret most about my life. Even though they hide a lot of things about their lives from me, I can see they need my help. I miss them so much—especially my mother. I remember she would always make special vegetarian food for me because as a boy, I couldn't eat fish or meat without becoming sick. As my brothers and I grew up, I remember her face always being so sad with worry for our future. The day I left to escape, she wanted to cry, but she hid her sorrow from my face. My mother's parting words to me were: "Now you're on your own. Live to make people happy. I won't be around. When the country becomes peaceful again, come back and see us. Remember, to make people love you is difficult, but to make people hate you is easy." My father rarely spoke, but as I left he told me, "I know you're still young, but I know you will grow with your life, because I believe in you."

Even with all the things I miss, I do not regret leaving my country. There was no future there for me. Here I can enjoy freedom and the chances there are to improve life—like being able to go to college and obtain a degree. When I look back over my life, I feel I have accomplished a lot, and I'm happy about it. But still there is a lot ahead for me to do. I must study more and obtain a good job so that I can continue to build my future. I especially want to earn enough money so that I can go home and see my family in Vietnam. If I always remember what I have done to get here and how hard I have struggled, I will attain that which my heart most desires: happiness.

Chapter 17
My Name Is William, but Call Me Bill

Nhut Q. Huynh settled in Woodford, Vermont, working for Nastech, a Japanese manufacturer of columns for Toyota, Mazda, Nissan, and Honda. He is married, has two children, and likes to fish and hunt.

In October 1980, when I was 16 years old, my father had made arrangements for us to escape from Vietnam. My mother woke early and made breakfast in the kitchen for us: rice soup, salty eggs, salty pepper (*dua mam*), and coconut rice (*xoi dua*). The night before, I had heard her footsteps as she walked up and down the stairs.

My father broke the news to us when we had our meal: "You have to take care of each other. We won't be around for you. I know how hard it must be when you're living in a foreign land, but you must be strong. I hope this situation is just temporary, and soon you will be home. Do the best you can."

I put my bowl of rice soup down on the table. I felt something stuck in my throat. My mother's eyes turned red. She looked down at the floor, then got up and went back into the kitchen. I wanted to cry, but I didn't dare cry in front of my father. That was the last time I saw my parents.

I followed my sister Kha, my brother Minh, and my nephew Phong with a few others to Vung Liem to meet the taxi that would deliver us to a woman's house. This woman would see that we got to a small boat that would take us to a bigger boat that was waiting somewhere on the Mekong. We pretended to be locals, so we carried oranges, mangos, and

158

a can of condensed milk as if we had been to the market. The designated taxi met us at the bus station and took us to the woman's house across the river from Vung Liem market. We had to hide in her house and be very quiet. In the afternoon she fed us vermicelli with boiled pork. Her daughter, Nhung, about 17, became our guide; she showed us what to do and where to go. When the sky turned dark and the woman was sure no one was around, she signaled for us to move to a thatched house near the river, where she had anchored the small boat, ready for the trip to the larger boat. But before we could leave, it started to rain and a V.C. [Viet Cong] showed up at the front door.

"Thiem Tu, Thiem Tu," the V.C. called out, "is Nhung home?"

He looked into the house to search for Nhung. I was behind the bamboo partition. I couldn't move my feet. They were stuck to the ground. I am dead, I thought.

"Nhung isn't home. She just went to town a few minutes ago. If you run you may catch her," Thiem Tu yelled in the rain.

She walked faster to the front of the house to prevent the V.C. from coming farther in. She met him and exchanged a few more sentences. Then the V.C. ran out of the yard into the dark.

I heard the sound of his footsteps pounding on the ground as if it were my own heart. Thiem Tu waited for a few minutes and told me to go while she was watching the road in front of her house. I darted onto the trail to the thatch house in the direction of the river. When I arrived, there was only one canoe left with four people it. Thiem Tu was behind me.

"Get on. Hurry before he comes back," she whispered to me.

After I got on, Thiem Tu pushed the canoe out into the current and jumped on. I helped her row. The boat moved quickly along the line of trees beside the river. We had traveled for about 20 minutes when I saw a flashlight shining into the water. It turned off and on four times. Thiem Tu aimed the canoe in the direction of the flashlight and rowed faster. After we reached the big boat, which was hidden in bushes, she held the canoe beside the boat and we climbed into the second boat. Someone on the boat reached out to pull us up. We did everything in silence in the dark. Thiem Tu didn't say a word. Finally, she pushed her canoe back into the river and left. Someone started the engine, and the big boat moved out toward the Ben Gia estuary. I took a deep breath and exhaled. My sister called our names in a whisper to make sure all of us were on the boat. I responded and tried to console myself with the thought that at least I had some relatives with me. I wondered about my parents, if they were asleep or if they were worried to death about us. I wondered why we had to leave our family and our country. What is my guilt?

Our journey went smoothly on the ocean. We had enough food and water for the whole trip. When we first reached the sea, we got on the deck to get fresh air. When my sister got seasick, she vomited and vomited. The sky was blue without any clouds. The water was peaceful, like a blue carpet. I heard the water washing gently against the boat. I saw a few dolphins racing beside our boat as if they cheered and welcomed us to their territory. Mr. Hai, our captain, knew exactly where we were. He told us how long it would take us and when it would be time for us to arrive in Indonesia. He had gone this way before, in April 1975, but the people on his boat had forced him to return to Vietnam. He had been in a concentration camp until just a few months earlier, when he was recruited by our boat owner. He knew this ocean well and how to avoid pirates. He aimed our boat directly toward the Galang refugee camp.

It took four nights and five days for the captain to get all 72 of us safely to Kuku Island. We stayed there for two months and then moved on to Galang. We received canned foods, hot dogs, instant noodles, and Spam. The officials assigned one barrack to a whole family. The concrete building looked like it belonged on a military base, but we had a convenient place to sleep with a bathroom, a kitchen, and running water. My sisters and brothers took care of me like my parents had in Vietnam, but I missed my mother and father and home. I wanted to go home, but I didn't tell anyone. I cried at night when nobody saw me.

First we signed up for an interview with the U.N. High Commissioner for Refugees. Then we had an interview with the U.S. officials. Since we had brothers in the States, we would automatically get to go to the States and be reunited with them. I took an English class to study American culture and the English language. It was very hard for me to understand. Besides attending classes, I played ping-pong and volleyball.

When I got sick of eating canned food, I asked my brother to go hunting for octopus, crabs, and fish in the ocean. I prepared a sharp metal stick, tied it onto a long bamboo branch like a spear, and got a string. Then I asked my brother Minh and my nephew Phong to swim to a small island about half a mile from Galang to hunt for fresh seafood. Although I swam just along the shore, the water was deep. I couldn't reach the bottom; but I could see all the way down. I spotted an octopus fanning the sand with his arms. I aimed my spear at him and pushed it into the target. Then I saw the dark ink released by the octopus. When I surfaced with my prize, Phong and I yelled out, "Look at this enormous octopus." My brother swam back to share our victory. I helped Phong tie a string around the octopus, then we moved to another area. We walked along the shore and went around the rocks and sand to look for clams and crabs. We caught a lot that day, and my sister cooked a wonderful meal for us with the fresh seafood. I ate and slept well that night.

One day my brother-in-law discovered some woods up in the mountains where there were many durian trees bearing fruit. He and I took a plastic bag and a knife and went back to the woods. I saw many durian fruit that had fallen on the ground. The fragrance was floating in the air. It smelled so good. The fruit looked like a porcupine because it had thorns all over it. My brother-in-law broke it with a knife, and we ate the layer wrapped around the seed. It tasted so good. I ate until I couldn't walk. When I came to the States, I bought durian at an Asian market and took it home to share with my wife and children. They told me it was stinky and tasted horrible. I was disappointed because it didn't taste like the fresh ones from the trees in the mountains.

After a year in Galang Camp had passed, the paperwork was completed and we had our physicals and shots, and it was time for us to leave the camp. In November 1981, I left with my brothers and sisters for Texas. First we went to Singapore and stayed in a refugee camp for one week. Then we flew to Tokyo and then Seattle. I first saw snow at the airport. It was so beautiful, as white as my grandfather's hair. I was amazed. When we arrived at the Dallas Fort Worth Airport on November 30, 1981, my brother Tuong came to pick us up. Everything seemed so big—the airport, the airplanes, the cars, and the highways.

I was scared. I didn't know much English even though I had studied it in the camp. I didn't know what was going to happen to me. How was I going to survive in this new society? I knew one thing for sure: I couldn't have cockfights as I had back in Vietnam because when I came to my brother's house, I didn't see any chickens in the backyard. He didn't have any dogs either. I saw that the grass in the front lawn and around the house was smoothly trimmed. The weather was different from that at home also. My brothers and sisters were happy, and they talked nonstop. They talked about my parents, the refugee camp, and everything they could think of. I met my four nephews and had a hard time understanding them, since they couldn't speak Vietnamese very well and I couldn't speak English.

My brother Tuong took me to the supermarket and showed me around. He explained how to shop for food and how to pay for it. He told me about one time when his family had not had food to eat for a few days. After he had received his paycheck for $65, he took his family to the market. His wife left the money in her purse in the cart while looking for an item. When she returned to the cart, her purse was gone. They went home empty that day and could only wait for the next paycheck. They were crying but didn't know where to turn for help. I was scared before, but now I was even more scared.

In Vietnam I could eat even if I didn't have any money. I could jump into the river to fish. I could catch snakes, rats, bats, or birds. At home when I caught a rat and cleaned it, my mother would marinate it with lemon grass and salt, then roast it over the fire. I ate it with jasmine rice. This was my favorite meal. Sometimes my mother marinated it with fish sauce, a dash of sugar, and black pepper. She let it sit for half an hour, then fried it until the meat turned brown. After she added coconut juice, she would let it simmer until the juice turned into liquid. It was a meal for poor people, but I never wanted to exchange it for anything at all. In Vietnam I could go to my uncle's or aunt's to eat if I wanted to, but here in America, if I didn't have food to eat or money, what could I do? There was no one I could turn to, and I didn't know enough English even to begin. I feared that there was no future here for me.

A few days later my brother took me to the Health Department for a checkup, then to the Welfare Department to apply for food stamps, since we had so many people in the family and my brother Tuong could not feed us all. My sisters and my brothers went to look for a job at Tandy and at my brother Tuong's company, Hitachi. Job hunting was made even harder because we had to find transportation. After a few weeks, when no one had had any luck, all of them except my nephew Phong and me moved to California with my brothers Lan and Ngoc. Tuong took us to Oakwood Junior High School and registered us for classes. I had a very hard time at first because the school system in this country was totally different from that in Vietnam. I had to search for my classes every period here, whereas in my country we stayed in one class and had only one teacher. Here I had many teachers in one day. I couldn't remember anyone's name at all. Whenever anyone introduced himself to me, he might say, "My name is William, but call me Bill," or "My name is Robert, but call me Bob." I was confused. How could I study English? Although I had extra help once a week, I couldn't get better. I felt isolated because I couldn't talk to anybody. There was too much pressure, not only from home but also from school, so I withdrew. I wanted to go back to Vietnam. I wanted to know what I was doing here in the first place. My job had been to bring my brother Minh safely to the United States, and I had. Why couldn't I go home? I wanted to make my parents and my brothers and my sisters proud of me, but I didn't know how. I didn't want to be a failure.

I stayed with my brother Tuong until June 1983, then moved to California. There were more Vietnamese in San Jose, and I liked it, but my brother Ngoc wanted to find a place to call home so that we could find peace to study. In July Ngoc, Minh, my nephew Phong, and I packed our sleeping bags, clothes, dry food, and instant noodles into the trunk of a 1967 Pontiac Firebird and headed east. I didn't know where we were going. It was hot, and the dirt rose like a small tornado along the road and on the highway. It was blurry, just like our future. We crossed the California state line into Nevada, then Utah, Wyoming, Nebraska, Iowa, Illinois, Indiana, Ohio, Pennsylvania, and New York, and finally drove to Bennington, Vermont. When the Pontiac broke down, we rented a shabby apartment and settled in.

We applied for welfare, and Minh, Phong, and I went to Mt. Anthony Union High School, where we met our counselor, Joan Costin, who helped us out. She looked after us like her own family. Ngoc worked at St. Peter's Church for Father Costin as a janitor, then later went to Bennington College on a full scholarship in September 1984 and moved into a dorm. He came to our apartment once every other week to visit.

At Mt. Anthony Union High School, I met a girl named Robin Hollister, and I fell in love. I started to think about her more than my homework and classes. I hung out with her and her friend and went to her house often, and from time to time I slept over at her place. On December 5, 1985, Robin gave birth to our boy, Nicholas. I graduated from high school, but I had no chance of going to a college or university. We were so poor that we lived in a rented trailer. I asked my sisters and brothers for money all the time. They often helped me, but I never had enough money to pay them back.

On June 4, 1988, my wife gave birth to another boy, and I named him Vinh. He had a big hole in his heart, and his face always looked pale because his heart wasn't pumping properly. When he turned five, his heart was operated on successfully. Vinh became normal and developed steadily, as a boy should. I was very happy.

Since 1991, I have been a Lead Tech for Nastech Company. Nicholas is in the seventh grade now, and Vinh is in the fourth. They are doing very well in school, and I am proud to be their father. I have been thinking of going back to Vietnam to visit my parents, since they are now so old, but I haven't had the money. I hope to take a trip soon, before it is too late. I didn't really know how to appreciate them when I was at home. But now, after having children of my own, I realize how much my father and mother loved their children and how much they gave up when we left Vietnam.

Chapter 18

Live Free or Die

Khon Luu and his son, Tam Luu, escaped by boat from Vietnam on November 23, 1987. Khon Luu settled with his family in Concord, New Hampshire. In 1990 Khon helped to found the Vietnamese Mutual Assistance Association of Manchester, and he was elected its first president. He was also instrumental in organizing and arranging Manchester's first Vietnamese New Year's celebrations. Since arriving in the United States in 1988, Khon has reunited with his wife, Nguyen Thi Ngoc, and their daughter, Chi Que. Today, Khon is a U.S. citizen who is happy for his freedom and believes in the future, not the past.

My name is Khon Luu. The word "Khon" means "wise"; "Luu" is my family name and was also the name of an ancient Chinese emperor of the Lesser Han Dynasty, "Luu Bi." Luu Bi lived during the Tam Quoc Ky ("Three Kingdoms Period") when China was divided by kingdoms and war. I too lived in a divided country—a country divided by competing foreign ideologies and war. In Vietnam, names have a purpose. Our parents select names that they feel will meet the personality of their child. The name also signifies what they want us to become. When I fled my country, I did grow into mine. I had no choice but to become "wise."

Ironically, although I am the grandson of Chinese immigrants who had come to the "Land of the Far South" looking for a better life, I too would have to leave my homeland in order to live. It burned my heart to leave, and the path to that life was a watery one—an ocean of tears.

I was born on March 5, 1953, the Year of the Snake, and grew up in Saigon's sister-city, Cho Lon—Vietnam's Chinatown. Anything Chinese, whether from the mainland, Taiwan, or Hong Kong, could be found in Cho Lon. Before 1975, it was a very noisy, bustling place. After 1975, most of its Chinese residents were being pressured to leave. Some felt they had no choice but to flee by boat. It was the Vietnamese government that encouraged the Chinese to get out.

My ancestors had come from a small village in Quang Dong Province, China. My father, Luu To, and my mother, Duong Thi Ngung, were middle-class people who lived a simple life. We never wanted for anything, and my brother and I were able to go to school and have a normal childhood. My father drove a taxi for a living while my mother was a homemaker who sometimes sold odds and ends in the marketplace. Although my parents spoke fluent Cantonese, I couldn't and had grown up speaking only Vietnamese.

Vietnam's history has always been one of fighting against invasion from the north or west, mixed with periods of relative quiet. Under the French, Vietnam had been split into three parts: Tonkin (the North); Annam (the Central): and Cochin (the South). Before the French, Vietnam had been split into two competing dynasties. However, Gia Long had reunited the country, only for it to fall to the French. The French treated us as second-class citizens and mobilized the three parts of Vietnam into work camps. It was only a matter of time before Vietnam fought back.

Although we wanted a united Vietnam, after the French were forced out, the North turned Communist under Ho Chi Minh while the South became a republic. The French had turned the South over to the Nguyen emperor, who ruled from Hue. But he wasn't popular. Soon after Vietnam was free, the emperor, Bao Dai, gave up his throne, and the first president of the Republic of Vietnam was sworn in. Soon after the Communists took over the North, we learned how difficult life was under their regime. A million Northern refugees fled across the DMZ [demilitarized zone] into the South. They didn't want to live under the repressive Northern regime.

The Southern government was in a difficult position. The Communists were planning to infiltrate the South and reunite all of Vietnam. The government in the South turned to America for help. I joined the South Vietnamese Air Force in 1971. I did so in the belief that I would do my part to help to protect my country against the Communist North. Yet I also feared that the Communists would win. Outside the city, the Communists were popular with the peasants. It was easy for the Northerners to win the war because nobody really knew who the Communists were. You couldn't tell by looking at them. It was easy, though, to spot and target the Americans.

During the war I was a sergeant in the South Vietnamese Air Force and worked as a fireman. I was stationed at two different bases—one near in Pleiku and the other outside of Saigon at Bien Hoa Air Base. After joining the Air Force I went to Pleiku, which is where I met my wife, Nguyen Thi Ngoc.

As the war wore on and life became harder and harder, I began to realize the South would lose. The Americans had pulled out, leaving the South to dangle in front of the tigers. It was inconceivable why they had gotten involved in the first place, only to pull out before they finished. I guess I don't blame America or the soldiers who came to Vietnam. I blame the policymakers who didn't know Vietnam in the first place and then didn't stick with what they started. They were just playing politics. America wanted to help Vietnam but did it in the wrong way. Although the Americans pumped money into Vietnam, corruption and the fact that they weren't Vietnamese meant they wouldn't win. How could they? Americans couldn't win against guerrilla warfare. The Americans would have to kill everyone to force the Vietnamese to do things their way. The Americans supplied us with every possible gun, machinery, anything you can name. The problem was that the equipment needed new parts. Where did we have to go get them? America. We became dependent on American aid. The American government helped Vietnam, it's true. But the way they helped was the problem. They wanted us to follow the American Way. But we weren't American. Our traditions were different. Our values were different. Our experiences were different. In the end, all the Americans did was make us dependent on them. This made many Southerners mad. The common Vietnamese in the South didn't like how their leadership followed America. We just wanted help, not for someone to push us around. The French had done that; so had the Chinese and the Japanese. None of them had succeeded. We all knew the Viet Cong would win, but we tried to delay it as long as possible. That's all we could do, delay. When the Americans pulled out of Vietnam, I felt bad because America didn't want to help our country anymore. Suddenly, we were alone against a powerful enemy.

Before the Northerners took over the South, my life had gone along well. Although the war disrupted our lives to some extent, it wasn't until the Communist victory and the fall of Saigon in 1975 that I realized how much I had before the South was lost.

When the Northerners poured into Saigon in 1975, my earlier involvement with the South Vietnamese and the American military impaired my chances for employment. Additionally, education for my children was also restricted. Hopes for a higher education for them would be just a dream. Life was totally changed for my family and me.

After the fall of Saigon, the new government wanted to send me and my family for "reeducation" at one of the New Economic Zones near the Cambodian border. These were places with poor soil, little food, and no medicine. To avoid this, my family went underground, just like so many others did in the same situation. I got myself another identity. But it was only temporary. They were bound to discover my trick.

The Northerners wanted to control everything. If you wanted to visit a relative outside the city, you needed permission. They stopped people to check us for the simplest reasons. Naturally, because of my prior military involvement, I was watched by the police and had to report any place I went. Then they put the pressure on so that I was barely able to do anything at all. In the end, to support my family, I used my pedicab to drive customers. I also traveled throughout the Camau Peninsula to sell whatever I could. I also fixed machines, anything to make some money to buy rice. My wife also had to support the family by selling fish. After Vietnam invaded Cambodia to punish the Khmer Rouge for killing Vietnamese civilians in Chau Doc, she sometimes went to their big lake, Tonle Sap, to get fish to sell in Vietnam. However, we still didn't have enough money to live.

As life became more and more difficult, and I was unable to find work due to my military involvement, I made the difficult decision to leave my country. It wasn't an easy decision. Who wants to leave the country of their birth? But I had no choice. I tried about eight times to escape, but every time people found out, and we had to try again and again. It was dangerous. If I had been caught, I would have been put in jail or sent to a reeducation camp for years.

Before my final escape, my father died. It was heartbreaking for me to have to leave my mother behind. However, my younger brother was there to take care of her. I finally succeeded in escaping Vietnam on November 23, 1987. I paid $6,000 in gold so that my son and I could escape. I didn't take my wife and daughter because if we had been caught, we all would have ended up in jail. I also worried that if we were unsuccessful in reaching safety by sea, my whole family would die.

My son and I left Vietnam by the Saigon River on a small boat about 18 meters long, stuffed with 192 people. The boat was cramped beyond belief, but unlike other boat people, we had enough food. We were also fortunate in that we didn't have to stay out to sea too long. The weather was good, and the wind blew us south. Within six days we reached an oil rig inside Indonesian coastal waters. The oil rig workers took us to Kuku Camp, about two hours by ferry from Singapore.

Other boat people weren't so lucky. We all know the stories of how other boat people were out at sea for over a month, with no food or water.

Eventually many would die, or pirates would rob them of their last chopstick, raping the women and leaving the men for dead.

At Kuku Camp the living situation was not easy. There was never enough food. Sometimes we bargained or bartered with the locals for monkeys, fish, anything we could eat. Then we were transferred to Galang camp. I was able to work for the Indonesian people there. I sold tickets for people to watch videos. With this money I was able to supplement U.N. food by bartering with the local Indonesians. The camp had at one time supported 20,000 refugees, but by the time we came only 2,000 were left. We stayed in Indonesia for six months and were then transferred to Bataan Camp in the Philippines.

At Bataan we were taught survival English, as well as how to live in America. Life was not too bad, similar to that at Galang. We spent half the day studying and the other half performing assigned duties. While we sat in camp, I thought of life in America—how it would be, what the people were like, and how I could become rich. America was the land of plenty. Everyone knew it. It was a place where dreams were made, we were told.

Six months later the Wesley United Methodist Church in Concord, New Hampshire, sponsored us to come to America. It was actually a mistake because the church had been waiting for the arrival of a Romanian couple. The church decided to help someone else out in the meantime. We were fortunate and finally settled in New Hampshire in November 1988. When we flew into Boston, we had only a small duffel bag filled with our lives. For the first month we stayed with our sponsors from the church. Then the church found me a job at HMC Corporation at Contoocook. They also helped me to find a one-bedroom apartment in downtown Concord.

Concord had very few Vietnamese—or other Asians, for that matter. I guess there were fewer than ten Vietnamese in Concord at that time. I used to go to Manchester to meet with some of the Vietnamese living there. Several had been in camp with me when I was in the Philippines. It felt good to have a drink with them, eat Vietnamese food, talk about our experiences, and help each other cope with the stresses we had to deal with. Eventually more and more Vietnamese came to New Hampshire. I could have moved to Boston or Dorchester, where there were more Vietnamese, but I realized that if I did, I'd never learn English and would never make my dreams come true. Manchester eventually had more and more Vietnamese refugees. I felt happy to see people from my mother country. Those who have never had to leave their homeland can't understand how it feels to be able to meet and talk with people who understand their thinking and culture. But for those of us who are exiles, it is very important. It is like a lifeline to us.

We all shared hardships and adversity leaving the country we loved, the country of our ancestors. To leave our families, friends, and everything that we knew was one of the most difficult things that we had to do. Think about it: who would willingly give up their country? Nobody. Yet what choice did we have? It was either leave or be imprisoned.

I found the HMC job difficult at first because I couldn't communicate very well in English. Even the corporation was unsure of how I could work effectively. However, I forced myself to learn English and, with the help of friends and church members, was able to work well. Every night I would carry around a dictionary, picture books of everyday things with their English meanings, and a torn, worn-out English-Vietnamese phrase book. It's strange, you know. One day, I left my fat Vietnamese-English dictionary on my car seat. When I went out to get it the next day, someone had stolen it. I guess it was some kids in the neighborhood. It was shocking to me. Why would anyone want to steal a Vietnamese-English dictionary? Yet I've learned that sometimes young kids here do things to prove that they are daring. They didn't think of how badly I needed the dictionary for everything I did or of how much money I had to spend to get another one. I worked 16 hours a day, six days a week. On my free day I wanted to sleep or visit with friends. I didn't have time to go out looking for a dictionary to replace the stolen one.

As I said, it was very difficult for me to live in America at first. I had nothing to remind me of Vietnam. My apartment was bare except for the donated furniture and curtains. Eventually things came. My son made a jigsaw puzzle of palm trees and the ocean that he glued and put up on the wall. It reminded me of home.

When I first came to the United States, it was very hard to find the foods that I liked to eat, such as tripe, chicken and pork livers, hearts, and fish sauce. I missed my wife and daughter more than when I was in Indonesia or the Philippines. At least the landscape there resembled that in Vietnam. Here, everything was so different. And it was cold. Every day I would look at my wife and daughter's photo and feel sad to be so far away from them. English was also difficult to learn. There were too many words. Although I had studied English in Bataan, I couldn't even say "hello" when I arrived in America. It was frustrating. Then, when I did start to learn, I found other problems kept popping up. I had also thought that America was an open society and that people were frank with each other. However, I've learned that people often say one thing but mean another.

It was relatively easy for me to be accepted into the United States because of my connection with the U.S. Army. However, I knew it would not be as easy for my wife. I feared that she would probably have to go through the same perilous journey that I did. But first I wanted to try the Orderly Departure Program. The program usually took five years or more before families could be reunited. I was fortunate again. It did take five years, but it could have been longer.

Now my wife and daughter are here. Before they arrived, my life in America was just a refuge, not a home. Since my wife and daughter arrived, my house has become a home. Now I work in recycling at a software manufacturer named Compaq in New Hampshire. I have also been able to buy my own apartment house.

Now we can find everything, even in Concord. I like living in America for many reasons. I guess that the most important reason is that I'm happy for the freedom. There is no control over the people here. However, I am disappointed that people aren't more open and friendly. I can't talk with them because they don't want to talk to me. Also there is prejudice here. Americans often compare themselves with us. I've met people who are also jealous because we work hard and we have something. I had thought that the American people were hard workers. However, I've found that some people are slackers who just want to enjoy life without putting any effort into working. In my experience, many don't pay attention to their jobs. That has made it easy for us Asians to do well because we are taught to pay attention to detail. If we don't, we won't have anything.

A year ago I went back to Vietnam. It was the same and yet it was different. I am proud that my homeland is making progress and that the living standard is getting better. I want Vietnam to enter the world market and the government to be truthful with its people. I feel that since the Communist takeover, the Communist government has changed 70 percent for the better. In the future, if I feel that I would not be given a hard time by the Vietnamese government, I will return to live out my remaining days there. However, when I went back to Pleiku the last time, the officials there gave me a hard time. If this type of behavior continues, I wouldn't want to live there. My hope is for America and Vietnam to become good friends and for both countries to help each other.

Today, when we celebrate the Vietnamese New Year in New Hampshire, the South Vietnamese flag flies alongside the United States flag. Although I am happy my country is reunited under one flag, whenever I look at the flag of the South I think about all that was and all that could have been. So many people died on all sides. There were so many sacrifices. When the New Year's ceremony begins, we pray to the spirits of all who died in the war, that they may find peace.

Chapter 19

Return to Leam Sing Camp

Jade Quang Huynh is an assistant professor of English at Appalachian State University in Boone, North Carolina. He received his bachelor's degree from Bennington College and his M.F.A. from Brown University. He is the author of *South Wind Changing* (Graywolf, 1994) and coeditor of this volume.

"Sa wat dee ka," a stewardess greeted me as I stepped onto a 747 departing for Bangkok ("Krung Thep" in Thai). She folded her hands in a praying position, placed them in front of her chin and bowed.

"Hello," I said. I wanted to greet her in her own language, but I was afraid she would laugh at my broken Thai. My heart raced and my palms were wet even though the plane was air-conditioned.

The stewardess smiled, her eyes shining. She was in Thai traditional dress: silk sarong, light purple top, and a dark purple silk sash draped across one shoulder. She looked like a Thai princess displayed in a gift shop. The purple orchids on her uniform were the insignia of Thai Royal Airlines, and purple was always a symbol of the Thai monarchy. I smelled her lilac perfume.

I showed her my ticket, and she pointed to the left side of the aisle. "On your left, sir."

"Thank you," I said and walked down the aisle to look for my seat.

Her voice was soft and her language as familiar as if I had heard it just yesterday, yet 20 years had passed since I had escaped from Vietnam and found shelter at Leam Sing Refugee Camp.

Now I was on my way back to the camp to confront what I had left behind. I hoped to find an answer to whom I had become and how I could move forward, but the scar I carried from my experience as a refugee haunted me like my own shadow. My brother, Thomas, his wife, To Lan, and their friend, Thin, accompanied me on this 10,000-mile journey. Thin spoke Thai well.

I put a small satchel in the overhead compartment and took my window seat—17A. My traveling companions settled in the same row. We left the United States at 11:00 P.M. on July 24, 1998. I was restless. I walked around the aircraft. I asked for water, although I didn't need it. I just wanted to have a chance to talk to a stewardess and to ask more about Thailand, the "Land of the Free."

The crew served us three meals before we arrived at Bangkok International Airport at 9:20 the next morning. The flight took 24 hours, including one stop at Osaka, Japan. I was relieved when the captain announced we were landing. I looked out the window, and a whole new horizon opened. Rice paddies, coconut trees, banana groves, bamboo trees, green and brown patches, and a cluster of black clouds scattered here and there; then tall buildings, red brick roofs, and streets and cars appeared in front of my eyes. Rain sprinkled on the window and reminded me that monsoon season had begun. I smelled a different air, heavy and sticky. The jumbo jet touched down on the runway and slowly taxied to the designated gate.

"Welcome to Bangkok," the voice of a stewardess announced on the speaker. "Thank you for choosing Thai Royal Airlines. It's our pleasure to serve you. I hope you have a pleasant stay in Bangkok or wherever your destination takes you. We're looking forward to serving you again."

I released my seatbelt and stood up, gathering my belongings. Thomas, To Lan, and Thin got ready to leave the plane. They looked exhausted. I was tired but filled with anticipation.

"Twenty years ago, at this very airport, I departed, and now I return. It seems like the old days," I said to Thomas.

Thomas smiled, rubbing my head.

"Are you ready for Bangkok?" Thin asked. "Everything has changed drastically."

"I am ready, but I need food," I answered, rubbing my stomach. "Airline food is not satisfying."

The passengers became noisier, and we moved toward the exit. We got off the airplane and went to the Immigration Office and Customs to check out. Thin called for a taxi to take us to a hotel in town. We checked in and went for a ride around Krung Thep.

We found a decent local restaurant and went in for lunch. We ordered fish dishes: crispy ca ro, sour soup, and salty catfish. I tasted the tender fresh fish, done the way my mother had cooked it for me. It was spicy and satisfying. There were many vendors and businesses along the road: jewelry stores, restaurants, and fresh fruit stands with hundreds of tropical fruits such as pummelo, durian, jackfruit, mango, papaya, bananas, mang cau dai, and plums. There were too many cars in the capital. Everywhere I went, I smelled sewage and smoke. Most of the buildings and houses were modern. They were all built in the same style except for those in the old Siamese style. Residents ran their businesses on the first floors and lived upstairs.

Cars drove on the left side of the crowded streets and seemed to flow constantly. Whenever I crossed a street, I felt like a dog caught in the middle of the traffic. I feared the cars were going to collide head-on. By the time we returned to the hotel to rest for the night, streetlights were lit.

The following day, Thin rented a chauffeured van for 1,500 baht, about $48 American money. We headed for Chanthabury, the center of fresh fruit production for Thailand. We planned to stop at Thamai District to find Pongsak, a friend of mine who used to run Leam Sing Camp. When we were out of Bangkok, the scenery changed from a bustling, hustling, congested, and polluted city to lush, green countryside and an open sky. The sun shone on the asphalt road. A few black clouds moved on the horizon. Banana, coconut, durian, and lonigan trees traced their own silhouettes on the fertile farms and along the highway. Sweat glistened on my face and dripped into my wide-open eyes. It was hot, but I enjoyed it.

Four hours later, our chauffeur pulled into a parking lot with a sign at the front gate reading "Thamai Police Station." It drizzled, and my heart sounded with the rhythm of the rain. The air was still. Thin and I got out of the van and walked into the office. Thin spoke Thai with the policewoman at the desk. She wore a gray uniform with gold insignias on both shoulders; she had a smooth, pleasant face. I described to Thin who my friend was, and he translated for me.

"Pongsak is a policeman. He was in charge of the camp when I was there," I said.

I looked at pictures of officers hanging on the wall to see if my friend was one of them. I didn't see him.

The woman at the desk picked up the phone and dialed.

"No one here recognizes that name," she said, hanging up the phone. "I'll go and ask around." She stood up from her chair and walked into the hall behind a counter. I held my breath and hoped she would find my friend. I hadn't written or called Pongsak before I left the United States. I wanted to surprise him.

The officer returned and told me she couldn't find Pongsak. "His house burned down recently, and he moved somewhere around here, but I don't know exactly where," I said. "I have his old phone number here."

I reached for my address book in my pocket, opened it to K, and found his last name, Kasanothai. I showed it to her, and she called his house.

"His phone is disconnected," she said. "I am sorry."

I felt disappointed, but I didn't want to give up.

"Would you call an operator for information?" I asked. "I have come a long way to see him." The officer made a call again. Her face lit up. She hurriedly wrote down something on a piece of paper and called a third time.

"Pongsak is the new mayor of Nayai Am District. The Interior Department just transferred him here a few days ago. He is my boss, and he is coming to the station in 15 minutes to meet you," she spoke quickly, as if she had run out of breath. "I have to go to the gate and wait for him."

She picked up her cap and walked out of the office. As I paced back and forth, my heart raced. A few citizens sitting on a bench in the office looked at me curiously and listened attentively.

"She is in trouble. She's a police officer, and she doesn't know her own boss," Thin said, laughing. "In Thailand, the Interior Department appoints mayors and authorities for the city and town. They don't hold elections like in the United States," Thin continued. "You're a refugee, and you know an important person. I can't imagine."

"He's just a friend," I said, and I went to the gate to look for Pongsak.

Pongsak pulled his old, beat-up Toyota pickup truck into the parking lot where we had parked the van. As I approached him, he opened the door and got out. We looked at each other for a moment. His mouth dropped, and his brown eyes opened wide. Pongsak had fat cheeks, a high forehead, and black hair. One of his distinguishing features was a mole on the left side of his upper lip. He wore a bluish-gray uniform. The policewoman greeted him and quickly talked as if she were afraid I would take my friend away from her. I hugged Pongsak even though I knew it wasn't appropriate to do so in Thailand.

"Do you remember me, Pongsak?" I asked, releasing him.

"Who could forget you, Jade? You have the same smile, with baby cheeks, sparkling eyes, and dark hair. You look practically the same, except you're fatter now than when you were in the camp," he said in English with a heavy accent. I knew he was complimenting me when he said I looked fat.

"I was starving in the camp. What do you expect?" I said and burst out laughing. "If you kept me longer in the camp, I might have become a thin bamboo tree."

He turned to the policewoman to thank her. She bowed to him and went back to her office.

Pongsak and I got into the van. I introduced my brother, my sister-in-law, and Thin. We headed downtown to Chanthabury for lunch. We talked and talked about the old days.

"Oh, the monk we used to visit when you were here died three years ago," Pongsak said. "Do you remember him?" he asked. "The one who saved the Vietnamese boy who'd been bitten by a snake?"

"Yes," I answered, and fell silent. I knew he must have been very old, and I knew that even if he were still alive and I went by to visit, he wouldn't recognize me. Maybe I couldn't identify him either.

"What about the lady who ran a stand at the entrance to the camp?" I asked, waving my hands in the air. "I used to go to her to exchange currency when I received money from Thomas. I bought a toothbrush, toothpaste, sugar, fish, vegetables, and some treats."

"She's still alive and in her eighties. She built a house not too far from the camp, and her youngest daughter is running the stand, selling groceries and knick-knacks. If we have time, I'll take you there. She'll be happy to see you," said Pongsak.

"Did you receive many letters from refugees all over the world, Pongsak?" I asked.

"Yes, I received a bucket of letters, but I can't read them because they wrote them in Vietnamese. Maybe you can read them for me," he answered.

He reached for his wallet in a pocket and opened it.

"Sure, I'll read them for you," I said.

"What happened to your friend in this picture?" he asked, pointing to a man. Pongsak passed the photo around for Thomas, To Lan, and Thin to see.

I looked at the photo but couldn't recognize the person because the picture was wrinkled and the color was fading.

"I can't see it. Who's this?" I asked.

"Your friend who spoke English well, remember?" Pongsak insisted.

"Oh, Hanh! He emigrated to Germany, and I lost contact with him," I exclaimed.

"That's too bad! Good friends are hard to find," he sighed. "At least I still have you."

Pongsak directed the chauffeur to a seafood restaurant. We had our meal together and enjoyed each other's company. After we finished our lunch, we visited the biggest temple in Chanthabury, then drove to Leam Sing.

It is a small village on the coast, about 750 kilometers from the Cambodian border. When I left Leam Sing in 1978, I had traveled this dirt road. Now it was full of potholes. There were many shrimp farms along the road. Here and there houses were scattered, and once in a while a car passed. The rain started and stopped, as if someone were sobbing.

The chauffeur accelerated, and the van headed up the hill for a final stop at a parking lot next to the temple overlooking Leam Sing Camp. Beside the temple was the cremation house. It consisted of a tin roof held up by six pillars, with no walls, on an 1,800-square-foot cement floor. We hopped out, stretched our arms and legs, and inhaled some fresh air.

Pongsak and I walked into the center of the cremation house, where the living held ceremonies for the dead. This was the area where Thai officials and embassy consuls had met to handle paperwork, interviews, food distribution, and guests. A silo chimney in the cement bunker had released smoke when the local residents cremated a corpse. I had breathed the stench of burning flesh for days, and it had nauseated me. Day and night, I heard the drum procession and the monks chanting without missing a beat.

This was the very place I almost got shot because of a drunken police officer. I remember walking down the trail to my hut to retrieve a plastic bucket so that I could get some drinking water. From out of nowhere, someone pushed me from behind, and I slipped into the dirt on my back. A shot rang out. A Vietnamese boy my size passed me like a shadow. I looked up and saw my brother Lan push the policeman's gun aside and yell, "Run, run, the policeman is going to shoot you all!" I got up quickly and was ready to move, but I saw a middle-aged man fall down onto the ground and blood wet his back. I stepped up to help the wounded man while people ran in every direction. Lan saw me and shouted: "Go, go, get a Thai interpreter! Hurry." I ran into the camp to look for the interpreter and asked him to come to the office with me. The interpreter spoke with the policeman and asked him to call an ambulance. Instead, a taxi came and took the wounded man to the hospital. I wondered why the policeman was not nice like Pongsak. The situation between the police and refugees became tense because of the incident. I couldn't wait to leave the camp.

"Jade, this is the food distribution center where we first met, remember?" Pongsak asked, sketching with his hands in the air. "You looked like a wet dog, timid and hungry. I had to order the refugees to let you go to the head of the line so that you could get your rice first. You had just entered the camp, remember that, huh, Jade?" He looked at me and patted my shoulder.

"Yeah, I remember, and after a few months, I became a rebel. I escaped from the camp to the mountain to find durian fruits, and one of your officers caught me and brought me to you," I said. "You took me into your office and closed the door. You pretended to cane me, then let me go. We have a long history together, don't we?"

"Yes, we do. I can't believe that you grew up to be a gentleman. Who would have believed then that you would become a published writer and a professor?" Pongsak said. "How many people can do that in life? Now you can speak for the refugees, for your people and for your country. I am happy for you, Jade." He squeezed my hand.

Pongsak and I led the group down the dirt trail to the actual campsite—the cemetery. Leam Sing Refugee Camp was closed in 1981. There was no sign of refugees. No one recognized the camp now. Bamboo, shrubbery, and trees grew wild, as if they wanted to erase the past. The black plastic and bamboo hutches were gone, as if nothing had happened on top of these graves—my temporary home.

Every night, we had been forced to guard our home against Thai men who tried to sneak into girls' huts to rape them or take them away. We designed a system to alarm the refugees when we had invaders. We collected Coke and condensed milk cans and linked them with long wire. We fenced them around the huts. Whenever someone spotted a suspicious individual, he would pull the can chain, which made noises to wake everyone. One designated individual had to go to the police and report. The rest of the refugees had to bang on pots and pans or whatever made noise to intimidate the intruders. Many young men my age would pick up their bamboo sticks and gather at the Baptist church, where we met earlier in the evening, to check the perimeter. Sometimes we had to stay awake all night because of a drunk. We would catch him and send him to the police, but the police just released him. He came back to the camp again and again.

On the side of the trail an empty, stained, plastic bucket lay next to the well where I used to fetch water and shower at night. At the end of the trail, a new bridge had just been built for fishing boats to dock when they returned from the open sea. A few local residents sat along the edge of the bridge, fishing. The moist air washed over my face when I stepped on the bridge.

I counted 17 steps as I moved to the exact spot on the bridge where my boat had been docked when I arrived here on April 2, 1978. Refugees who had come to the seashore to greet us threw down bread, soda, water, and cookies. There was no bridge then, only muddy sand, rocks, and sharp mussels. I remembered the policeman shooting in the air because he wanted to scare us. Refugees coached us on how to guard ourselves and made a hole in the boat to sink it. The Thai boat was unable to tow our boat back to the open sea. The ones on the boat who had relatives living in the camp were the luckiest because they could ask their relatives to hold valuable provisions for them and send them supplies. We were stuck on the water for a few days until the U.N. High Commissioner for Refugees official arrived and let us enter the camp.

During the days at sea, the sky had seemed so high and I felt so small. The sun shone weakly, like an oil lamp running out of kerosene. I looked out into the ocean and saw an island growing out of the blue water where a red fishing boat appeared. The sound of the engine was familiar, and the blood red of the boat made me dizzy. Black smoke popped up and down from the boat, like a person struggling with asthma.

Somewhere out there beyond the island, about a day's travel by boat, I had lost the last battle to pirates. It was dark. Our rickety boat was heading to Chanthabury when we saw a boat with bright lights approach us. I thought it was our second rescue. The boat reached ours, and ten young men jumped over to our boat. "Police, police!" they said. They searched all of us and took watches, earrings, chains, and whatever valuables they could get. They looked in every corner of the boat. They threw our pots and pans back to their boat and disabled our engine. They shoved women and girls to one side of the boat and men and boys to the opposite side. Next thing I knew, there was a knife at my neck, and I saw the rest of my group being taken hostage. A Thai pirate stepped over to a girl and grabbed her. He yanked her blouse. The mother held his leg, and he kicked her. She stumbled onto the deck moaning. He shouted something to his boat, and suddenly the lights from the boat turned off and it became dark again.

"Help me! Help me!" the girls wailed.

I couldn't move. I was as helpless as the female victims. I grabbed the hand holding the knife to my neck and pushed it away with all of my energy. I quickly moved my leg to the side and elbowed the fake policeman in his chest. He lost the knife, and I bent my knees and swung him over my head. "Fight, fight. We'll only die once," I shouted as loud as I could.

I heard the commotion: pounding footsteps on the deck, paddles knocking on the boat, people groaning, and children crying. The lights from the Thai boat turned on again, and the engine was revving and aimed directly at our boat. Their boat crashed into ours. I lost my balance and slid into the water. I saw many shadows follow me. I pulled my arms through the water, but the waves pushed me away from my boat. The Thai boat turned off their lights again, and this time I heard the girls' yelling calm to a whisper. I don't know how long I was in the water; I just kept calling out to my friend to swim back to our boat.

No one answered me. Finally the lights turned on again, and the other boat sped away. I climbed back on board our boat and helped the women and children.

Fortunately, the Thais didn't kidnap anyone. Women wrapped up the naked girls, and as I watched them, my soul died. We assisted our wounded comrades, salvaged what we had left, and rowed the disabled boat toward the shore, far, far away. I knew we were headed in the right direction, but I didn't know if Thailand was the right place for us. Maybe it was better for us to die at sea. I felt the irony because our first rescue had been by another Thai fishing boat, whose crew had saved us from the middle of nowhere in the ocean. They fed us, fixed our boat, and towed it to the Chanthabury region. They put us back into our boat, gave us food and water and diesel for our engine, and pointed to Chanthabury. I wondered whether it was worth it to trade for our freedom. I felt a chill. There was no sound except our paddles clanking at the side of the boat.

At the end of the horizon, I knew it was Vietnam. I was so close to home, but I couldn't live in my own country. I closed my eyes and breathed.

"Where is the camp?" Thomas asked, interrupting my train of thought and returning me to the present.

I opened my eyes, looking up toward the cliff. At the end of the cliff, a green mountain range rolled like a giant wave where a red roofed temple stood still like nothing mattered. A dragon statue on the roof was in position ready to catch his prey.

"Right there," I said, pointing to the surroundings at the end of the bridge, "on top of the graves along the cliff. At the hump of the green spot was the Baptist church where I used to come waiting for your letter every week. You see those tall trees on the mountain and the glistening leaves waving back and forth? They are durian trees," I continued, pointing to the spot in the distance. "The camp is empty now, but you can't imagine how noisy it was then. You don't really see the camp, do you?"

"No, I don't," Thomas said, adjusting his glasses. "But I see it in a way."

If Thomas couldn't see the camp itself, how could I trust my memories and senses? Maybe it was my illusion. I couldn't imagine what my daughter would see or think if I brought her here after she grew up.

Thomas turned to his wife and explained it to her.

Pongsak took some pictures for us. I walked off the bridge to the sand. Waves rubbed back and forth at my feet, sounding like bamboo leaves moving in the wind. The water was warm and seemed to be rising higher and moving farther inland. I inched closer to a bamboo grove and found a stone cross engraved in English and Thai. I read, "This place was once a temporary home, a camp for the Vietnamese boat people, refugees who fled their motherland from Communism seeking justice and freedom 1975-1981 AD." The refugees are always remembered, I thought.

"Jade, it's getting late. We have to go," Thomas called to me.

"Good-bye, Leam Sing." I mumbled to myself, looking at the surroundings one more time. My stomach felt squeamish, and my eyes blurred.

I brushed off my warm tears and went back to the trail to join the others. I got in the van and rode off to Chanthabury as if I were running away from my past.

The sun had already gone down, and the rain had stopped. Lights were lit here and there. People gathered inside their houses while crickets and frogs orchestrated the night. Everything around me—the sky, the air, the mountains, the sea, and the people—had changed, and yet they remained the same.

Again, I came to Leam Sing. Again, I left Leam Sing. But this time I came as a United States citizen and not a refugee. I don't know if it made any difference because I was still a refugee without my homeland.

Pongsak wanted me to stay longer. He invited me, Thomas, To Lan, and Thin to his house, the government quarters, but Thin had to go back to Bangkok for personal business.

"It's very nice of you, but I can't stay this time," I said, shaking his hand. "I shall return and live here in a few years. I hope your invitation will still be open then."

"Anytime, Jade. You're my friend," he answered with a cracking voice. He blinked his eyes.

We dropped off Pongsak at Thamai Police Station and said goodbye. He stood in the parking lot, waving his hand, watching the van disappear in the dark. My heart sank. I was quiet all the way back to Krung Thep, and a few days later I returned to America. My trip was completed, but my journey had just begun.

Appendix: UNHCR Statistics Concerning Indo-Chinese Refugees in East and Southeast Asia

The following statistics on Vietnamese asylum seekers were provided on 18 November 1997 by F. Fouinat, Director, Bureau for Asia and the Pacific, United Nations High Commissioner for Refugees.

1. Since 1975 to June 1996 a total of 839,228 Vietnamese asylum seekers were registered and assisted by UNHCR in refugee camps in countries of first asylum in Southeast and East Asia namely in Indonesia (121,708), the Philippines (51,722), Malaysia (254,495), Thailand (160,239), Singapore (32,457), Hong Kong/Macao (202,961), Japan/Korea (12,419) and other countries (3,227). During this period some 755,670 Vietnamese refugees were settled in third countries. Please refer to the attachment for details of resettlement countries.

2. The highest number of Vietnamese asylum seekers arriving in one year occurred in 1979 when a total of 140,436 arrivals were registered in UNHCR assisted refugee camps in South East Asia. This population included 55,705 in Hong Kong which was the highest number of Vietnamese arrivals in one country/territory in a year. Historical information on individual camps is not readily accessible, however,

we would endeavour to provide further details should specific camps and/or countries be of interest.

3. The Comprehensive Plan of Action for Indo-Chinese refugees (CPA), which was adopted in June 1989, established a framework for international cooperation at a time when asylum in South East Asia was in crisis. It reduced clandestine departures from Vietnam, expanded legal departure possibilities, and introduced region-wide refugee status determination procedures which helped to stem the flow of asylum-seekers. Under the CPA some 109,322 Vietnamese who did not fulfill internationally accepted refugee criteria repatriated to their country of origin. (Although the CPA was formally completed on 30 June 1996, repatriation of the remaining 22,000 Vietnamese in Hong Kong continued until June 1997). At present, 2,065 Vietnamese are remaining in Hong Kong, 1,650 in the Philippines, and less than 60 persons in other first asylum countries in Asia. Only one refugee camp known as Pillar Point in Hong Kong remains open.

4. With regard to the treatment of returnees upon return to Vietnam, UNHCR has financed 800 small infrastructure projects to improve the living conditions of the returnees and the local communities within which they have reintegrated. In conjunction with this assistance UNHCR monitoring teams have visited some 40 percent of all returnees. The great majority of returnees were found to be integrating satisfactorily. None were suffering from discrimination or ill-treatment as a consequence of them having left their country illegally. A limited number of arrest cases were related to criminal offenses prior to departure from Vietnam. UNHCR intervenes effectively to assist returnees who experience difficulties, most often with regard to the renewal of their residence rights or relating to administrative difficulties in obtaining their repatriation entitlements.

RESETTLEMENT DEPARTURES BY COUNTRY OF RESETTLEMENT DURING THE MONTH.
CORRESPONDING CUMULATIVES FOR CURRENT YEAR AND FROM 1975 UNTIL PRESENT.

HONG KONG

COUNTRIES OF DEPARTURE	VIETNAMESE TOTAL MONTH	VIETNAMESE TOTAL 1997	VIETNAMESE CUMULATIVE TOTAL
AUSTRALIA	1	2	10,272
BELGIUM	0	0	225
CANADA	0	25	26,131
DENMARK	1	1	1,603
FINLAND	0	0	559
FRANCE	0	5	2,274
GERMANY	0	0	2,545
JAPAN	0	0	628
NETHERLANDS	0	0	1,067
NEW ZEALAND	3	3	942
NORWAY	0	1	1,074
SWEDEN	0	0	1,364
SWITZERLAND	0	0	723
UNITED KINGDOM	23	27	15,640
UNITED STATES	244	253	71,358
OTHERS	2	6	2,140
TOTAL	274	323	138,545

INDONESIA

	VIETNAMESE TOTAL MONTH	VIETNAMESE TOTAL 1997	VIETNAMESE CUMULATIVE TOTAL
AUSTRALIA	0	1	21,641
BELGIUM	0	0	189
CANADA	0	0	16,452
DENMARK	0	0	306
FINLAND	0	0	170
FRANCE	0	0	2,334
GERMANY	0	0	2,524
JAPAN	0	0	246
NETHERLANDS	0	0	472
NEW ZEALAND	0	0	619
NORWAY	0	0	387
SWEDEN	0	0	783
SWITZERLAND	0	0	652
UNITED KINGDOM	0	0	113
UNITED STATES	0	0	64,840
OTHERS	0	0	148
TOTAL	0	1	111,876

JAPAN

COUNTRIES OF DEPARTURE	VIETNAMESE TOTAL MONTH	VIETNAMESE TOTAL 1997	VIETNAMESE CUMULATIVE TOTAL
AUSTRALIA	0	0	722
BELGIUM	0	0	132
CANADA	0	0	735
DENMARK	0	0	62
FINLAND	0	0	3
FRANCE	0	0	81
GERMANY	0	0	34
JAPAN	0	1	3,593
NETHERLANDS	0	0	45
NEW ZEALAND	0	0	40
NORWAY	0	0	695
SWEDEN	0	0	1
SWITZERLAND	0	0	71
UNITED KINGDOM	0	0	112
UNITED STATES	0	1	3,978
OTHERS	0	0	46
TOTAL	0	2	10,350

KOREA

	VIETNAMESE TOTAL MONTH	VIETNAMESE TOTAL 1997	VIETNAMESE CUMULATIVE TOTAL
AUSTRALIA	0	0	71
BELGIUM	0	0	20
CANADA	0	0	64
DENMARK	0	0	0
FINLAND	0	0	0
FRANCE	0	0	72
GERMANY	0	0	39
JAPAN	0	0	10
NETHERLANDS	0	0	109
NEW ZEALAND	0	0	231
NORWAY	0	0	87
SWEDEN	0	0	5
SWITZERLAND	0	0	1
UNITED KINGDOM	0	0	5
UNITED STATES	0	0	663
OTHERS	0	0	10
TOTAL	0	0	1,387

MACAU

COUNTRIES OF DEPARTURE	VIETNAMESE		
	TOTAL MONTH	TOTAL 1997	CUMULATIVE TOTAL
AUSTRALIA	0	0	536
BELGIUM	0	0	5
CANADA	0	0	2,295
DENMARK	0	0	66
FINLAND	0	0	0
FRANCE	0	0	77
GERMANY	0	0	12
JAPAN	0	0	31
NETHERLANDS	0	0	4
NEW ZEALAND	0	0	30
NORWAY	0	0	21
SWEDEN	0	0	497
SWITZERLAND	0	0	103
UNITED KINGDOM	0	0	179
UNITED STATES	0	0	3,678
OTHERS	0	0	174
TOTAL	0	0	7,708

MALAYSIA

	VIETNAMESE		
	TOTAL MONTH	TOTAL 1997	CUMULATIVE TOTAL
	0	0	48,540
	0	0	516
	0	0	33,874
	0	0	727
	0	0	672
	0	0	6,867
	0	0	4,352
	0	0	435
	0	0	1,867
	0	12	1,621
	0	0	854
	0	1	1,508
	0	0	2,838
	0	0	451
	0	0	142,079
	0	0	1,580
	0	13	248,781

PHILIPPINES

COUNTRIES OF DEPARTURE	VIETNAMESE		
	TOTAL MONTH	TOTAL 1997	CUMULATIVE TOTAL
AUSTRALIA	0	0	6,355
BELGIUM	0	0	97
CANADA	0	0	5,573
DENMARK	0	0	245
FINLAND	0	0	7
FRANCE	0	0	3,284
GERMANY	0	0	1,648
JAPAN	0	0	823
NETHERLANDS	0	0	596
NEW ZEALAND	0	0	384
NORWAY	0	0	624
SWEDEN	0	0	385
SWITZERLAND	0	0	407
UNITED KINGDOM	0	0	409
UNITED STATES	0	0	28,047
OTHERS	0	0	675
TOTAL	0	0	49,559

PRTC
(Ex – Hong Kong only)

	VIETNAMESE		
	TOTAL MONTH	TOTAL 1997	CUMULATIVE TOTAL
	0	1	1,244
	0	0	2
	0	0	1,998
	0	0	38
	0	0	0
	0	0	50
	0	0	0
	0	0	53
	0	0	309
	0	0	14
	0	0	140
	0	0	798
	0	0	214
	0	0	3
	0	0	878
	0	0	0
	0	1	5,741

THAILAND

COUNTRIES OF DEPARTURE	VIETNAMESE BOAT PEOPLE			VIETNAMESE LAND PEOPLE		
	TOTAL MONTH	TOTAL 1997	CUMULATIVE TOTAL	TOTAL MONTH	TOTAL 1997	CUMULATIVE TOTAL
AUSTRALIA	0	0	14,657	0	5	2,344
BELGIUM	0	0	148	0	0	323
CANADA	0	0	11,355	0	0	3,118
DENMARK	0	0	435	0	0	117
FINLAND	0	0	393	0	0	52
FRANCE	0	0	3,406	0	0	5,663
GERMANY	0	0	1,427	0	0	1,360
JAPAN	0	0	128	0	0	86
NETHERLANDS	0	0	515	0	0	234
NEW ZEALAND	0	0	490	0	0	483
NORWAY	0	0	690	0	0	118
SWEDEN	0	0	228	0	0	163
SWITZERLAND	0	0	464	0	0	426
UNITED KINGDOM	0	0	726	0	0	96
UNITED STATES	0	16	72,694	0	4	22,568
OTHERS	0	0	365	0	0	601
TOTAL	0	16	108,121	0	9	37,752

COUNTRIES OF DEPARTURE	LAOTIAN: LOWLAND			LAOTIAN: HIGHLAND		
	TOTAL MONTH	TOTAL 1997	CUMULATIVE TOTAL	TOTAL MONTH	TOTAL 1997	CUMULATIVE TOTAL
AUSTRALIA	0	0	8,949	0	0	1,290
BELGIUM	0	0	977	0	0	12
CANADA	0	0	16,301	0	0	973
DENMARK	0	0	0	0	0	12
FINLAND	0	0	6	0	0	0
FRANCE	0	0	26,005	0	0	8,231
GERMANY	0	0	1,681	0	0	25
JAPAN	0	0	1,254	0	0	19
NETHERLANDS	0	0	33	0	0	0
NEW ZEALAND	0	0	1,283	0	8	67
NORWAY	0	0	2	0	0	0
SWEDEN	0	0	26	0	0	0
SWITZERLAND	0	0	568	0	0	25
UNITED KINGDOM	0	0	346	0	0	0
UNITED STATES	8	134	122,249	1	281	129,085
OTHERS	0	0	4,227	0	0	461
TOTAL	8	134	183,907	1	289	140,200

THAILAND

COUNTRIES OF DEPARTURE	CAMBODIAN			TOTAL: THAILAND		
	TOTAL MONTH	TOTAL 1997	CUMULATIVE TOTAL	TOTAL MONTH	TOTAL 1997	CUMULATIVE TOTAL
AUSTRALIA	0	0	16,298	0	5	43,538
BELGIUM	0	0	745	0	0	2,205
CANADA	0	0	16,805	0	0	48,552
DENMARK	0	0	31	0	0	595
FINLAND	0	0	37	0	0	488
FRANCE	0	0	34,206	0	0	77,511
GERMANY	0	0	874	0	0	5,367
JAPAN	0	0	1,058	0	0	2,545
NETHERLANDS	0	0	464	0	0	1,246
NEW ZEALAND	0	0	4,243	0	8	6,566
NORWAY	0	0	126	0	0	936
SWEDEN	0	0	17	0	0	434
SWITZERLAND	0	0	1,637	0	0	3,120
UNITED KINGDOM	0	0	273	0	0	1,441
UNITED STATES	0	0	150,226	9	435	496,822
OTHERS	0	0	8,043	0	0	13,697
TOTAL	0	0	235,083	9	448	705,063

REGIONAL TOTAL

COUNTRIES OF DEPARTURE	VIETNAMESE BOAT PEOPLE *			VIETNAMESE LAND PEOPLE		
	TOTAL MONTH	TOTAL 1997	CUMULATIVE TOTAL	TOTAL MONTH	TOTAL 1997	CUMULATIVE TOTAL
AUSTRALIA	1	4	108,808	0	5	2,344
BELGIUM	0	0	1,729	0	0	323
CANADA	0	25	100,012	0	0	3,118
DENMARK	1	1	4,592	0	0	117
FINLAND	0	0	1,813	0	0	52
FRANCE	0	5	21,421	0	0	5,663
GERMANY	0	0	15,489	0	0	1,360
JAPAN	0	1	6,388	0	0	86
NETHERLANDS	0	0	7,332	0	0	234
NEW ZEALAND	3	15	4,476	0	0	483
NORWAY	0	1	5,950	0	0	118
SWEDEN	0	1	5,857	0	0	163
SWITZERLAND	0	0	5,814	0	0	426
UNITED KINGDOM	23	27	19,329	0	0	96
UNITED STATES	244	270	402,382	0	4	22,568
OTHERS	2	6	6,526	0	0	601
TOTAL	274	356	717,918	0	9	37,752

*Including Singapore

R E G I O N A L   T O T A L

COUNTRIES OF DEPARTURE	LAOTIAN: LOWLAND			LAOTIAN: HIGHLAND		
	TOTAL MONTH	TOTAL 1997	CUMULATIVE TOTAL	TOTAL MONTH	TOTAL 1997	CUMULATIVE TOTAL
AUSTRALIA	0	0	8,949	0	0	1,290
BELGIUM	0	0	977	0	0	12
CANADA	0	0	16,301	0	0	973
DENMARK	0	0	0	0	0	12
FINLAND	0	0	6	0	0	0
FRANCE	0	0	26,005	0	0	8,231
GERMANY	0	0	1,681	0	0	25
JAPAN	0	0	1,254	0	0	19
NETHERLANDS	0	0	33	0	0	0
NEW ZEALAND	0	0	1,283	0	8	67
NORWAY	0	0	2	0	0	0
SWEDEN	0	0	26	0	0	0
SWITZERLAND	0	0	568	0	0	25
UNITED KINGDOM	0	0	346	0	0	0
UNITED STATES	8	134	122,249	1	281	129,085
OTHERS	0	0	4,227	0	0	461
TOTAL	8	134	183,907	1	289	140,200

R E G I O N A L   T O T A L

COUNTRIES OF DEPARTURE	CAMBODIAN			GRAND TOTAL *		
	TOTAL MONTH	TOTAL 1997	CUMULATIVE TOTAL	TOTAL MONTH	TOTAL 1997	CUMULATIVE TOTAL
AUSTRALIA	0	0	16,309	1	9	137,700
BELGIUM	0	0	745	0	0	3,786
CANADA	0	0	16,819	0	25	137,223
DENMARK	0	0	31	1	1	4,752
FINLAND	0	0	37	0	0	1,908
FRANCE	0	0	34,364	0	5	95,684
GERMANY	0	0	874	0	0	19,429
JAPAN	0	0	1,061	0	1	8,808
NETHERLANDS	0	0	465	0	0	8,064
NEW ZEALAND	0	0	4,426	3	23	10,735
NORWAY	0	0	128	0	1	6,198
SWEDEN	0	0	19	0	1	6,065
SWITZERLAND	0	0	1,638	0	0	8,471
UNITED KINGDOM	0	0	273	23	27	20,044
UNITED STATES	0	0	150,241	253	689	826,525
OTHERS	0	0	8,063	2	6	19,878
TOTAL	0	0	235,493	283	788	1,315,270

*Including Singapore

Index